FINE
KAHN

Art of the
APOLOGY

How, *When*, and *Why* to
Give and Accept Apologies

Lauren M. Bloom, J.D.

Fine & Kahn

New York

FINE
KAHN

Published by Fine & Kahn, LLC
322 Eighth Avenue
New York, NY 10001

Art of the Apology
LC Control Number: 2013942713
ISBN 978-1-937075-00-2

A previous edition of this book, *The Art of the Apology*, was published by
Green Angel Media, LLC, in 2008.

Published by Fine & Kahn, LLC

Printed in the United States of America.

Fine & Kahn and the Fine & Kahn colophon are registered trademarks.

QF   10   9   8   7   6   5   4   3   2   1

For everyone who ever had to make an apology . . .

in other words, for almost everyone.

CONTENTS

INTRODUCTION

Since childhood, I've been a passionate lover of the performing arts, enjoying music and theater both as a performer and as a delighted audience member. One of my favorite high school roles was Lucy in *You're a Good Man, Charlie Brown*, a musical comedy based on Charles Schulz's much-loved comic strip *Peanuts*. In a most memorable scene, hotheaded Lucy storms onstage and informs her brother Linus that their mother has cancelled Lucy's birthday party because Lucy has misbehaved. Linus sensibly suggests that Lucy apologize to their mother, providing a little speech that begins, "I'm sorry, *dear* Mother." Lucy agrees to try it, and manages to struggle through almost to the end before turning to Linus and bellowing, "I'D RATHER DIE!!!"

That scene drew an appreciative laugh from the audience and especially amused my mother, who happily quoted that speech for years whenever we had an argument. There were moments when I was very sorry I had ever played the part in front of her, but that speech is the only thing in the show that I remember decades later. Even then, I could see the value of a good apology.

I've since grown up, gone to law school, and spent twenty-five years working as an attorney. I've counseled dozens of clients through professional crises, argued in front of federal judges, and spent hundreds of hours educating professionals on good business conduct. I've been married and divorced, changed jobs several times, traveled extensively at home and abroad, held friends' hands through their personal troubles, read dozens of self-help books, and watched people interact in settings from the highway to the boardroom as they struggled to get along.

Based on all those experiences, I've come to one inescapable conclusion: Nobody's perfect.

As fallible human beings, we're bound to make mistakes. If such a notable as Saint Paul could lament, "That which I should do, I do not—that which I should not do, I do," what hope do the rest of us have of getting through life without doing something wrong now and then? We lie, we procrastinate, we break promises, we make unkind remarks or stupid jokes, and we step on each other's toes every single day. And, unless we do something about it, our relationships with the people around us suffer for it.

The secret, when you make a mistake, is to apologize.

Unfortunately, many people find making an apology downright painful. They would rather go to the dentist for a root canal than apologize for something they've done wrong. It's not that they're coldhearted. It's usually that they're embarrassed, uncomfortable, or unsure of what to say. They find it's easier to shrug it off, make a joke, hope the whole problem will just go away over time, or even end a relationship altogether than it is to go to someone they've angered or hurt and apologize.

This book is intended to help you think about the importance and value of apologies, and to learn how to apologize effectively to practically anyone. Apologizing can be difficult, but it's essential to maintaining successful relationships and a civilized society. Unless you're prepared to change jobs on a regular basis and replace your friends once a year and your spouse once a decade, learning how to apologize effectively is an essential skill at work, at home, and in life.

In the chapters that follow, we'll discuss the reasons to apologize and when and how to do it. We'll look at how apologies need to differ in different settings, and why the way you apologize to a business associate is not the way you apologize to a friend or loved one. We'll look at the most common mistakes people make when they apologize, and identify ways to avoid them. We'll examine alternatives in situations in which you can't bring yourself to apologize, and we'll address the special challenges that accompany having to apologize for a really spectacular blunder. Finally, we'll talk about how to accept an apology in a way that leads to true forgiveness and stronger relationships.

Throughout this book, you'll find stories about how people dealt with various situations in which an apology was in order. These are true stories involving friends, colleagues, and clients that I've encountered over the years. I've changed their names and, in some cases, altered the facts a little to protect the privacy of the people involved. These stories are intended to demonstrate the fine art of the apology, illustrating how to apologize and some of the pitfalls to avoid.

Inspirational author Margaret Lee Runbeck once wrote, "Apology is a lovely perfume; it can transform the clumsiest moment into a gracious gift." I hope you will use the ideas in this book to make your own life, and those of the people around you, a little more gracious.

HOW TO USE
THIS BOOK

This book is intended to help you apologize in a wide range of situations and to many different kinds of recipients. I recommend that you sit down and read it from beginning to end *before* you start using its advice. You may be tempted to "skip and dip" through the book—skip to the chapters that are most applicable to your particular situation and dip into only those parts, where you'll find the advice that is most likely to be useful to you. Unless you're already experienced at the how to apologize artfully, I'd advise against this. Reading the whole book will help you familiarize yourself not only with the principles of effective apologies, it will give you a thorough understanding of how the process of apology works in various situations.

Once you've read through the book and successfully followed its advice once or twice, you may thereafter be able to refer only to particular chapters that relate to a particular situation. The one that will apply most frequently when you find the need to apologize is Chapter 3, "The Six Essential Elements of an Effective Apology." As the title suggests, the elements identified in this chapter should almost always be taken into consideration if you want an apology to be effective, regardless of who the recipient is or why you're apologizing. Until you know all six of the essential elements by heart, it's probably a good idea to review Chapter 3 every time you have an apology to make. It's your apology Bible.

May your apology be graciously received and accepted.

PART ONE

BEFORE THE APOLOGY

CHAPTER 1

Why Apologize at All?

Of all acts of man repentance is the most divine. The
greatest of all faults is to be conscious of none.

—THOMAS CARLYLE

There are many reasons people refuse or fail or are reluctant to apologize when they've offended someone else. Pride, embarrassment, anger, shame, or the fear of losing an advantage or of being unfairly punished can all create a nearly irresistible temptation to say no to saying you're sorry. It's so much easier just to hope that time will heal the damage you've done or to walk away from someone who deserves an apology. This chapter will help you understand why apologies are so often the necessary and right thing to do.

Common Reasons Not to Apologize

It's no surprise that people are so often reluctant to apologize: There seem to be so many reasons to avoid it. Here are some of the reasons people hesitate to apologize—and explanations of how those reasons don't hold water.

I'm too embarrassed. Some mistakes are particularly humiliating to the people who make them, and that feeling can make it tempting to hope that the whole thing will simply blow over if it isn't brought up again. "I can't believe I was so stupid," one man lamented after drinking too much at a company party and making a foolish remark to his boss's wife. "She'll never forget what I said, my boss will never forgive

3

me, and I'll never live it down," he continued. "I might as well just find another job right now. It would be a lot less painful." This man clearly believed that no apology could restore his reputation—in essence, he believed that other people would never forgive him, because he couldn't forgive himself. The incident did happen, though, and the failure to acknowledge it didn't make it go away. Maybe the man's boss won't forgive him, but he'll never know, and probably never rest easy about it, if he doesn't apologize for his offensive behavior.

I don't know what to say. Even when people want to apologize, they can't always find the right words. "I'm absolutely mortified," one teacher said after learning that a student he had scolded in front of the class for being late with a paper was suffering the emotional side effects of her parents' messy divorce. The teacher wanted to apologize but was afraid that no matter how he worded it, he couldn't help but embarrass the student by implying that her family's private problems were known around the school. "It's probably best not to say anything at all—she'll get over it, and I'll know to be more careful from now on," he reasoned. While his intention to do better in the future was a good one, the teacher's failure to apologize cast a shadow over his relationship with the student and her classmates that lasted throughout the school year. It's almost always better to apologize than to let bad feelings fester, even if the apology is imperfectly phrased.

Apologizing will make me look weak. Some people fear that if they admit to an error and apologize, others will see their error as a flaw or weakness. "Me, apologize?" a supervisor once said about his abusive treatment of an employee who had made a mistake in an important report. "I'm the boss here, and I handle my employees the way I see fit. If that idiot doesn't like being told when he's screwed up, he can quit!" He was afraid that if he acknowledged his bad temper, his employees would respect him less. The trouble is, people know when someone has made a mistake or behaved badly. Refusing to acknowledge an error or apologize for it makes a person look arrogant, stubborn, and immature. Apologizing after a mistake is a sign not of weakness but of maturity and strength.

The recipient will never let me live it down. Sometimes people are reluctant to apologize because they see an apology as the beginning of a long, hard penance. "I'm not going to apologize," a friend recently said about a cruel joke he'd made about his wife having gained some weight. "She'll never let me forget about it if I ever admit I was wrong." He was afraid that his wife would use his apology as a weapon for months, if not years, to get the advantage in future disagreements. Small wonder he was hesitant to admit that he had been unkind. Unfortunately, by failing to apologize he dealt his wife a second insult, implying that she was too self-righteous and vengeful to accept his apology with grace. Apologies to those we are closest to can be especially sensitive (we cover that in Chapter 8, "Apologizing to Loved Ones"), but it's damaging to the relationship and downright hurtful to withhold a deserved apology from someone you love.

Some people aren't worthy of apologies. Sadly, a common excuse is grounded in the attitude that workplace subordinates simply aren't important enough to deserve apologies. When called on the carpet by his boss for having submitted an inflated expense report, Joe blamed the mistakes on his secretary, Alice. He later heard through the grapevine that Alice had learned what he'd done and was upset about it. Joe didn't apologize, rationalizing that "taking the fall for her boss is part of her job description." He was genuinely puzzled when she quit a few weeks later. Co-workers who are subordinate to you in the office hierarchy deserve to be treated with the same respect as your peers and superiors. We'll talk more this in Chapter 6, "Apologies in the Workplace," but suffice it to say that withholding apologies from those who are beneath you in the hierarchy can do tremendous damage to office morale and personal success.

I haven't done anything wrong. Sometimes, people refuse to apologize because they believe they're in the right. "Why should I apologize?" one woman asked after chewing out her daughter-in-law for her messy housekeeping. "Their home is a pigsty, and my poor son can't so much as find a pair of clean socks that match. She deserves every word I said!" This woman wouldn't admit that although she was right that the house could use some attention, the way she made her point was hurtful to her long-term relationship with her son and his wife. It wasn't what she said as much as the nasty tone with which she said it that caused the hurt feelings. It would have been far better for the woman to apologize for being judgmental and harsh than to let her self-righteous behavior create a lasting rift in the family.

The stakes are too high. Part of making an effective apology is taking responsibility for your actions, but that can be scary if the consequences associated with your mistake loom too large. A business analyst who had recommended that his corporation purchase a small competitor later realized that he had seriously understated the risks associated with the acquisition. He was terrified of being fired if he admitted to the error and apologized, so he chose to say nothing and hope things went well. In such situations, though, a failure to admit to a mistake can seem like an intentional cover-up after the fact. It's almost always better to apologize for a mistake when you discover it than to have to explain later why you failed to do so.

I might get sued. With the risk of lawsuits constantly escalating, many businesspeople and professionals avoid apologies for fear that they'll become the basis for lengthy, expensive litigation. Philip, a pediatrician, made a mistaken diagnosis that almost cost one of his young patients her life. The girl survived, but only after suffering a long and painful illness. Philip wanted to apologize to the girl and her family, but his lawyer advised against it. "I'm afraid they're going to sue you for malpractice," she warned. "If you admit you made a mistake, you'll be handing them an easy victory in court." The lawyer's advice may have been prudent, or not—we'll explore that point in greater depth in Chapter 7, "Apologizing in Business (and Why Your Lawyer May Object!)"—but it did nothing to heal the relationship between Philip and his patient's family the way an apology might have. In fact, a national movement is under way to encourage doctors to apologize for errors without increasing their legal liability, and some studies even show that an apology can actually reduce the likelihood of a lawsuit.

Reasons to Apologize

Given all the reasons not to apologize, why do it at all? The answer may depend on the circumstances: what you did, why you did it, who you did it to, how they felt about it, and what it will mean for you in the future if you don't say you're sorry. Ultimately, though, there are at least seven very good reasons to apologize to someone when you've done something wrong, even if you'd really rather avoid it, and other people are encouraging you not to bother.

You're genuinely sorry. The best and most straightforward reason to apologize is that you're sorry about something you've done and want to make things right. While there can be practical reasons you might be reluctant to apologize, or others might argue against an apology, it's important not to let those practicalities distract you from your fundamental sense of right and wrong. When you hurt or offend someone else, apologizing for what you did is simply the right thing to do.

To maintain good relationships. Apologies can do a world of good for all of your relationships. If your business colleagues, friends, and loved ones know that you are someone who openly admits to your mistakes and tries to make amends, they'll respect, trust, and love you more. Communication among you and others will be better and more relaxed, because hurt feelings will be less likely to fester. Over time, you will find that your own self-respect and happiness will increase. Saying "I'm sorry" once in a while is a tiny price to pay for all those big, beautiful benefits.

To salvage a relationship. If the person you've hurt is important to you, whether personally, professionally, or otherwise, blowing off a deserved apology is a great way to risk losing that person's trust and goodwill. If you've built a sufficiently strong relationship with that person in the past, he or she may forgive you—once, anyway—if you hurt or offend him or her and fail to apologize. Do it repeatedly, however, and you're setting up a disaster with someone who matters to you.

William was a brilliant organizational psychologist, who was intelligent, well read, and articulate. Unfortunately, he passionately enjoyed debating almost every point and, in his eagerness to demonstrate his intellectual superiority, often slipped from debating into bullying in conversations with his wife, Dorothy. When she complained that some of his tactics were too aggressive, he would dismiss what she said, loftily informing her that she was being too sensitive and needed to be more open to other people's opinions—specifically, his. Dorothy tolerated William's behavior for years but eventually found his domineering impossible to live with and filed for divorce.

If William had respected Dorothy as much as he valued his own debating prowess, he might have been receptive enough to her feelings to realize he should apologize to her when his eagerness to win a point got out of hand. As it was, he succeeded in winning many arguments with her, but lost his marriage in the process.

To contain an escalating crisis. Sometimes an apology is the best way to keep a tense or difficult situation from spiraling completely out of hand. A well-timed and delivered apology can prevent a labor strike, head off a riot, save a marriage, salvage a friendship, or preserve a family. Even (or perhaps especially) if there's wrong on both sides, one party usually has to say "I'm sorry" first before reconciliation is possible. Often, all it takes after a fight is for one person to say, "You know, I'm really sorry," to open the floodgates of apology and reconciliation.

Connie was an administrative assistant who worked for a branch office of a cable company. A white woman from a small southern town, she was extremely uncomfortable with having her "personal space" invaded. A few years after she came to work in the office, the owner hired a new general manager, Ron, to oversee the staff. Ron, from New York City, was an outgoing, warmhearted African American man who routinely bear-hugged his friends, stood close in conversation, and patted his employees on the arm or shoulder when giving them direction. Connie couldn't stand Ron's style, characterizing it as "in your face," but she was too shy to ask Ron to step away and stop touching her when he talked to her. She grew increasingly unhappy and angry about Ron's "invasive" behavior, finally filing a sexual harassment complaint against him.

Ron was flabbergasted. He had no idea that he had been making Connie uncomfortable, and he was hurt and angry that she hadn't talked to him before filing the complaint. He felt that she had been dishonest with him, and suspected that her actions were racially motivated because no one else had complained about him and she was, after all, from the South. Within days, Ron had become as upset as Connie was.

Fortunately, the office's human resources director contacted the company's attorney. They investigated the situation and decided to try to avert a full-scale lawsuit. They explained to Ron that, while his actions had not been intentionally offensive, he had violated Connie's comfort zone. They appealed to his good nature, pointing out that he was the supervisor and, therefore, had more responsibility for keeping the peace in the office than Connie did. Although he was upset at first, Ron recognized that apologizing to Connie would be a good way to prevent a painful and expensive lawsuit, and he agreed to make the apology. The human resources director then spoke with Connie. She explained that Ron had not realized that he was making Connie uncomfortable, and encouraged Connie to speak up in the future when she was feeling uneasy. She then asked Ron to come in, and Ron apologized to Connie. Things were a little awkward for a week or so, but Connie ultimately dropped her lawsuit and worked well with Ron thereafter.

Ron's willingness to apologize defused a potential disaster. He learned from the apology (something you'll learn more about in Chapter 18, "Learning from Your Apologies"), and was more careful afterward about how he related to his staff. Connie, in turn, learned that she could trust management, and particularly Ron, to listen to her concerns and respond respectfully. She became more trusting, and her work improved. The result was multifold: Ron's apology led to a happy, productive workspace.

To benefit someone else. In some situations you might have to look past yourself and the person you've hurt or angered in order to find a reason to apologize. Even if the injured person isn't especially important to you, he or she is almost certainly important to someone else. You may not care much whether that person ever speaks to you again. But if you care about someone who cares about that person, you may find that an apology is a small price to pay for great results.

Sally couldn't stand Mark's mother, Eleanor. She was rude, narrow-minded, bigoted, and cold. However, Sally loved Mark deeply, and when he proposed to her, Sally instantly said yes, dreaming of their wonderful life to come. She forgot that Mark came with a family—in particular, with Eleanor.

Sally's daydreams hit a wall of reality as the wedding plans were announced. Eleanor had an opinion about everything, and she wasn't the least bit shy about sharing her views with everyone. She complained about the wedding date, the location, the invitations, the color scheme, and so on, until Sally couldn't stand it anymore. One day, when Eleanor was holding forth about her disappointment with the dinner menu for the reception, Sally lost her temper, called Mark's mother an unprintable name, and stormed off sobbing. Truthfully, Eleanor wasn't unhappy about Sally's outburst—it gave her the perfect opportunity to add another complaint to her ever-lengthening list of disappointments. She seemed to take particular pleasure in telling anyone who would listen that Sally had insulted her, that Sally was unstable, and that Mark was making a tragically inappropriate choice.

Mark, on the other hand, was devastated. He knew that his mother could be opinionated and unpleasant, but he loved her and felt responsible for looking after her, particularly because his father had passed away. He felt torn between his love for Sally and his loyalty to Eleanor. For a while, it looked as though the wedding might never take place.

Sally would have been quite content never to see Eleanor again. She didn't like or trust her future mother-in-law and she felt as though Eleanor had goaded her into losing her temper with the unending flood of criticism. Nevertheless, when she thought things through, Sally realized that Mark was so important to her that she was willing to make peace with his mother to please him. This was not an easy thing to do. Almost everyone who knew them thought that Eleanor's behavior had been outrageous and silently cheered when Sally told her off. But Sally was mature enough to take the long view and realize that the immediate gratification of asserting herself was not worth sabotaging her relationship with Mark.

Sally was afraid to apologize to Eleanor in person—she feared that Eleanor would try to take the upper hand by criticizing Sally until another explosion occurred. Instead, Sally wrote a personal note and attached it to a bouquet of flowers that Mark delivered on her behalf to Eleanor's house.

It was a classy, elegant gesture, and it worked. Eleanor was mollified, Mark was relieved, and the wedding proceeded on schedule. Sally learned from the experience. She put a little distance between herself and Eleanor, and reminded herself regularly that she was in love with Mark, not his mother. Her apology to Eleanor proved to be the best wedding present Sally could have given to her husband-to-be.

To preserve your own integrity. Chicken maven Frank Purdue joked in one of his commercials, "It takes a tough man to make a tender chicken." To paraphrase, it takes a courageous and humble soul to apologize for a regrettable act or behavior. Courage and humility are two of the greatest virtues, and practicing them will, ultimately, make you a stronger and better person. When you know you've behaved badly or hurt someone's feelings, it's perfectly normal to feel ashamed and a little embarrassed. Pretending the whole thing never happened can seem like a very attractive alternative, but you know it's not honest, and it won't repair your relationship with the person you've offended. When you've made a mistake, square your shoulders, admit to what you've done, and apologize. You'll find the restoration of your personal integrity worth any fleeting embarrassment.

To contribute to making the world a better place. While there can be many good reasons to apologize in a particular situation, perhaps the best reason is that apologizing when you've made a mistake helps restore civility to the world. Apologies are about courtesy and treating other people with respect and kindness. Every sincere apology contributes to making the world a kinder, more pleasant place and offsets some of the stress and rudeness that so many people object to today.

Why Are *You* Apologizing?

There are many good reasons to apologize, but before you issue an apology to anyone, it's important to consider and understand your intentions. You need to be clear in your own mind about your motivations before you open your mouth to someone else. Otherwise, you run the risk of doing or saying something that will make the situation worse. When you were a child, you may have been ordered by a parent, teacher, or other authority figure to apologize to someone for something you said or did. "You shouldn't have kicked Johnny in the knee—now, go on, say you're sorry!" The reluctant "I'm sorry" you managed to mumble in Johnny's general direction may have mollified your mother, but you and Johnny both knew you were only apologizing to get out of trouble. That sort of apology may work on the playground, but it's certain to be a flop from one adult to another.

Why *are* you apologizing? Maybe it's because you're genuinely sorry and want to ask the person you've offended to forgive you so that you can stay on good terms. If that's the case, great! It will be easier for you to apologize because you won't have any internal conflict about it, and you won't need to worry about sounding insincere.

If, after you've read this chapter, you're still not so eager to say you're sorry, ask yourself these questions:

- Even if I don't really want to apologize for what I did in this situation, is the other person important to me? Will apologizing help me keep on good terms with him or her? Would I be sorry if I let this relationship deteriorate to the point where it vanished?

If so, isn't it worth making an apology for the long-term health of our relationship?

- Is this a potentially serious situation? Am I looking at a possible lawsuit, the loss of my job or professional credentials, a divorce, or an equally devastating outcome? Could an apology prevent that disaster, or at least increase the chances of resolving the situation short of a trip to court? If so, isn't it worth a try?

- Even if I'd be thrilled never to see the other person again as long as I live, is that person important to someone else who *does* matter to me, like my parent, child, best friend, significant other, or boss? Will it make things easier for my loved one if I apologize? Will my loved one be forced to choose between me and the other person if I don't apologize?

- Did I really mess up? Did I do something so dishonest, hurtful, stupid, or thoughtless that I'll be unable to think about it without being embarrassed or upset? Will apologizing clear the decks and help me recover my self-respect? Will it help me regain the respect and trust of the people around me?

- Did my actions create or contribute to an untenable situation? Will apologizing for what I've done help restore peace and goodwill to my family, my workplace, or my community? Will apologizing reinforce my personal integrity and restore my self-respect?

If the answers to those questions don't help you decide to apologize, ask yourself this: *If I don't apologize now, will I look back on this situation weeks, months, or years from now and wish that I had?*

If your answers to these questions, and particularly to the last one, amount to "yes," you need to apologize. The good news is that you know now why you're doing it. Your next step is to decide what to say. The next several chapters will help you do just that.

CHAPTER 2

Think Before You Speak

*Look within. Within is the fountain of good, and
it will ever bubble up, if thou wilt ever dig.*

—Marcus Aurelius

Once you've decided to apologize to someone, it's tempting to just do it. Don't! A few minutes of careful thought and planning are essential to making your apology as successful as it can be. Take a moment, take a breath, and think about the following five questions.

What Did You *Really* Do?

It's impossible to make an effective apology if you don't fully understand—or own up to—what happened. While you might think what happened is obvious, consider that it's all too easy to let your pride or embarrassment distort your perceptions. It's important to get your facts straight, so try not to let your emotions mislead you. Above all, don't get defensive.

When you know you've done something wrong, it's usually embarrassing. Consequently, it can be terribly tempting to minimize what happened in your own mind so you can feel better about yourself. Resist that temptation—it will lead you to a halfhearted apology that won't do the job and may do more harm than good.

Take a long, hard look at what happened. Be brutally honest with yourself. In particular, examine your motives. Let's say you offended another person: When you did so, were you acting out of ignorance, or was it thoughtlessness? Were your actions planned, or were you acting on impulse? If you didn't mean the other person any harm, you probably have less to apologize for than if you had acted intentionally. On the other hand, if a dark little corner of yourself really wanted to hurt the other person, you need to acknowledge that ugly truth, at least to yourself. There are two extremely good reasons to do this. First, you need to be aware of what your motives were, so that you can decide what to say when you apologize. Second, if you don't figure out why you wanted to hurt the other person, it will be only a matter of time before you do something else to him or her and find yourself having to apologize again. *Wanting* to hurt someone isn't necessarily unforgivable—in fact, it can be a reasonable response in some circumstances. It's actually *doing* it that you want to avoid. Keep in mind that if you deliberately hurt someone else or if your behavior gave you an unfair advantage over a competitor or if what you did injured someone particularly innocent or helpless, you're going to have to work that much harder to apologize effectively.

Likewise, even if your transgression wasn't against a particular person, your motives have a lot to do with how serious of an act it was. If, for example, you accidentally took five extra dollars out of the petty-cash box in your office because two bills stuck together, it almost certainly won't be a big deal to apologize and return the money. If you took fifty dollars from petty cash intending to return it after payday without asking permission first, that's worse, but since you didn't actually steal the money you can probably apologize and be forgiven, especially if you have a good track record otherwise and vow not to do it again. But if you took fifty dollars from petty cash and submitted a phony expense voucher to cover your theft, you're in pretty serious trouble, because you have demonstrated intentional dishonesty. If you stole fifty dollars from the coffee can containing your colleagues' holiday donations to Save the Children, even apologizing might not save you from having to update your resume and clean out your desk. The amount of money may not have been any different, but your motive was so ugly that you'll have to make amends by taking your punishment without making excuses.

The famous twelve-step program developed by Alcoholics Anonymous requires people who want to be freed from addiction to alcohol to conduct a "searching and fearless moral inventory" of themselves. It may not be necessary to conduct a brutally honest examination of yourself every time you step on someone's toe or forget to return a library book, but unless you're sure that what you did was pretty minor, err on the side of caution and look hard at how you behaved.

At the same time, make sure that you don't dramatize. Some people are so sensitive about themselves that they see even the most modest slipup as a world-class disaster. If you're prone to that kind of hyperemotional self-flagellation, take a deep breath and get control of your emotions. You're apologizing because you offended *somebody else*. You'll benefit from making the apology, but this really isn't about you. Take a step back, and think about whether what you did was really all that awful, especially when compared to some of the really hideous things that people do to each other sometimes. If you don't get a reasonable perspective on the situation, you're likely to deliver such an overblown apology that you'll end up looking silly, self-involved, or both, and the apology won't be effective. Leave your inner drama queen behind.

Find the middle path. Since your goal in this step is to come to a clear understanding of what you did wrong and why you did it, the key is to find balance. Get to where you can acknowledge what you did without trying to hide it or blow it out of proportion. You're going to need to be able to discuss your actions when you apologize, so make sure you can describe them clearly, fairly, and honestly.

Why Are You Sorry—*Really?*

We've all heard politicians deliver public "apologies" for misdeeds ranging from taking bribes to seducing underage staffers. One of the traits that these so-called apologies often have in common is that, no matter how elegantly they're phrased, they often come down to, "I'm sorry I got caught, and I'm apologizing because my public-relations director told me I had to act contrite if I wanted to get reelected." We all know how utterly ineffective those apologies are (we talk about them in more depth in Chapter 10, "Public Apologies").

If the only reason you're sorry is because you got caught, you're nowhere near ready to apologize. As we'll see in the next chapter, sincere regret is an essential element of an effective apology. Take another look at what you did, and see what aspects of your behavior make you most uncomfortable when you think about them. You'll almost certainly discover that those sore spots point toward your most genuine regret. Maybe you're not sorry you inflated your travel expense report, because you think you're underpaid for the work you do—and you may even be right to feel that way. But if you're sorry that you violated your boss's trust and disgraced yourself in front of your business colleagues, those are very legitimate reasons for embarrassment and, not coincidentally, excellent reasons to apologize for your misdeed. We all want to look in the mirror and see someone we respect, someone who acts with honor and integrity. We also want to see someone other people respect and trust. If your actions blur that reflection, that's a valid motivation for wanting to apologize.

As we discussed in the previous chapter, however, there are many reasons to deliver an apology, and they don't all start with misconduct. If you're apologizing solely to avoid further trouble or to please someone else, chances are pretty good that you don't think you did anything wrong. Again, you may be entirely right about that, but you still have to apologize effectively if you're going to achieve your desired goal. To put it another way, before you can say you're sorry, you need to decide what you're sorry about. Think back and see if you can identify things that you might have done better, explained more clearly, said more gently, or handled with greater diplomacy. Even if you didn't do anything *wrong*, you didn't do everything perfectly right, because no one ever does. Remember, nobody's perfect. Don't beat yourself up unnecessarily, but acknowledge that you could have been clearer, more tactful, or better prepared, and that things might have gone differently if you had been.

Were There Mitigating or Aggravating Circumstances?

This step focuses not on your internal motives when you acted badly, but on external conditions that might have influenced your behavior. Think about what was going on in your life when you made your mistake. Were you under stress at home or at work? Had you gone too long without sleep or nourishing food? Were you lacking important information or laboring under a false impression? Would you have acted the same way if you were calm, rested, better informed, or less rushed?

The goal here is not to develop a string of excuses—nothing ruins an apology faster. The goal is for *you* to understand how your actions might have been influenced by circumstances beyond your control. This lets you do three important things. First, it can help you explain, not excuse, your behavior to the person to whom you're apologizing. Second, it can help you identify circumstances in your life that tend to push you into bad behavior, so you can change them or, at least, work to minimize their influence on you. Third, and maybe most important, it helps you learn from your apologies, so you're less likely to repeat the same transgression. (See Chapter 18, "Learning from Your Apologies," for more.)

It's not always easy to acknowledge outside circumstances that push you toward unkind, unwise, or thoughtless behavior. Losing a job, ending a marriage, fighting with a family member, financial worries, illness, and other stressors all take their toll. If you're too mortified to admit to the person you offended that you're going through tough times, so be it. Still, cut yourself a little slack when it comes to forgiving yourself: Remember, you're only human.

Sometimes, though, the circumstances surrounding your mistake won't help you. People can do hurtful or unethical things even when it seems as if everything is already going their way. (If you doubt that, just think about some of the news stories you've seen about über-rich investors who indulge in insider trading or sports stars who bet on their own games.) If it seems as if there were no outside factors at play when you acted badly, accept it and move on. There's nothing to be gained by reaching for empty excuses, and it can be wonderfully free-ing to admit that you, and you alone, are responsible for what you did wrong. If nothing else, it's easier to mend your ways if there are no outside obstacles standing in your way.

What Were the Consequences of Your Actions?

Think through the impact of what you did. How severe was the harm you inflicted? Is it temporary or permanent? Whom did you hurt? Bumping into someone because you weren't watching where you were going usually isn't terribly serious—but it is serious if you knocked the person over and caused her to break her wrist. Again, your culpability is a matter of degree. A frail elderly person might suffer more severe injuries from being knocked over than a healthy high school student would. When you're trying to answer this question, don't dwell too much on how the other person might have contributed to the situa-tion: You're still the one who needed to be more careful.

Give some thought to the permanency of the injury as well. Sadly, time doesn't necessarily heal all wounds, and it's a mistake to assume that hurt feelings or physical injuries will fade on their own.

It may seem impossible to apologize for doing significant harm, but even the most serious injuries can be forgiven. However, be sure you understand the impact your actions had on other people before you apologize, or you might do even more damage by making an apology that fails to acknowledge the seriousness of your mistake. (See Chapter 13, "Apologizing for a Serious Transgression," for more on what to do in grave situations.)

How Far Will You Go to Make Amends?

Once you've delivered an apology, you may have to take action to correct the mistake. Before you propose how you'll do so, decide how much you're willing to do to wipe the slate clean. If you've thought through what you did, what you're sorry about, what circumstances contributed to your mistake, and how much damage you did, you probably have a pretty good idea of what it will take to set matters to rights.

Deciding how far you're willing to go is important for several reasons. First, as we'll see in the next chapter, it can be very effective if, when you apologize, you tell the other person what you're going to do to make amends. You can't do that if you haven't thought it through beforehand. Second, if you're concerned that the other person will try to take advantage of you and demand more in restitution than you think is fair, you'll be more likely to avoid an uncomfortable situation if you take control and predetermine what actions you will take, rather than leaving things open-ended. Third, if you don't have a specific idea of what you'll do to make amends, the recipient of your apology may get stuck trying to figure out how you can make things right, and since the mistake was yours, it's hardly fair to place that burden on someone you've already injured. Lastly, if you take the time to decide how much you're willing to do to make amends and come prepared with a plan, it'll confirm to the other person how important he or she is to you and that you understand how serious your transgression was.

Before you go ahead and issue your apology, be sure you have honestly answered these questions for yourself:

- What did I do wrong? Do I really remember what happened? Am I getting defensive? Am I overreacting? What were my motives when I made the mistake? Did I do it accidentally or deliberately? Was I really intending to hurt the other person, or was I just thoughtless? When I apologize, how should I characterize my actions?

- Why am I sorry? Is it because I know I did something wrong, or just because I got caught? If I'm just sorry I got caught, how can I change my attitude? Do I even think I did anything wrong? If not, how could I have handled things better then, so I wouldn't have to apologize now? Am I genuinely sorry for that? When I apologize, what should I say I'm sorry about?

- What was going on around me when I slipped up? Was there anything happening that might help explain what I did? Without making excuses, is there anything I want to admit or explain to the wronged person that he or she doesn't already know?

- How much damage did I do? Was the injury relatively minor, or more serious? Will the passing of time take care of it, or did I do permanent harm?

- How can I make amends? What will I need to do? What time, money, effort, goodwill, political capital, or other resources am I willing to expend to correct the situation? At what point will making amends become too costly for me?

If, after going through these questions, you're still not clear about what happened and how you will proceed, ask yourself this: *What must I do to make things right, and am I willing to do it?*

Once you know the answer to that question, you're ready to start working on your apology. The steps for that begin in the next chapter.

CHAPTER 3

The Six Essential Elements
of an Effective Apology

Say you're sorry when you hurt somebody.

—ROBERT FULGHUM, *All I Really Need to Know
I Learned in Kindergarten*

Every apology is unique. An apology that works perfectly in one situation
may be totally inappropriate in another setting. When deciding what to
say when you apologize, think carefully about whom you're talking to,
what you're apologizing for, what you hope to achieve by apologizing, and
how the other person or people involved might respond. In later chapters,
we discuss apologizing in different settings and to different kinds of
people; those discussions are intended to help you deal with the specifics
of any situation in which you need to apologize.

There are, however, certain elements that are essential to almost
any effective apology. Depending on the circumstances, and particularly if you have a good relationship with the person to whom you're
apologizing, you may be able to get away with skipping one or more
of these elements. But if you want to be confident of achieving all
your goals, make sure your apology contains a healthy dose of all of
these elements.

Say You're Sorry, *Sincerely*

This is one element you absolutely can't afford to skip: Say you're
sorry—and mean it. Be direct, be honest, and don't get too fancy. If you
start going overboard with the violins, elaborate prose, and flowers, the

person you're apologizing to will likely think you're being sarcastic, patronizing, or just putting on a big show, and your apology will be a complete failure. Don't hesitate or qualify. Just say the words "I'm sorry."

In order to say them effectively, it's crucial to know exactly why you're sorry. Unless you're clear in your own mind that you're sorry for a specific reason, you won't be able to tell the other person why you're apologizing, and your apology is likely to sound phony, as though you're making it just to keep the peace and not because you really mean it.

If you're apologizing because you really want to or because you think it's the right thing to do, you probably won't have to worry about whether you sound sincere. On the other hand, if you're apologizing to avoid further trouble or to help someone else, be a little more careful to make sure your apology sounds genuine. Although you undoubtedly have a very sincere desire to resolve matters favorably, you may not be entirely sorry about what you did. Find the thing that you genuinely regret—causing the other person upset or inconvenience, creating bad feeling, generating a misunderstanding—and apologize sincerely for that. As the English writer G. K. Chesterton wisely said, "A stiff apology is a second insult. . . . The injured party does not want to be compensated because he has been wronged; he wants to be healed because he has been hurt." Take the time to find the words that will heal the other person; those words are essential to an effective apology.

Take Responsibility

Whatever you did that you're apologizing for, admit to it openly, and don't try to minimize it or blame someone else. Be direct, be truthful, and don't make excuses. Saying such things as, "It really wasn't that bad" or "It wouldn't have happened if Bob hadn't . . . ," will make it seem as though you're trying to wiggle out of your apology even as you're making it. Be particularly careful not to blame the person to whom you're apologizing. Even if you truly believe that the other person deliberately goaded you until you reacted and did something you regret, don't say so now. Pointing the finger will only make matters worse. If your apology goes well, you may have an opportunity to tell your side of the story—gently—afterward.

It's vital that you understand exactly what you did wrong so you can take responsibility for it. Once you know what you're apologizing *for*, you can figure out how to take responsibility for it in a straightforward way. As we discussed in Chapter 2 ("Think Before You Speak"), to arrive at this understanding you'll also need to consider what was motivating you when you blundered. Did you make an honest mistake, or did you deliberately do something wrong? If you intentionally hurt the person to whom you'll be apologizing, you'll probably have to admit to your harmful motives and apologize for those, too. On the other hand, if you were just thoughtless or clumsy, don't take on more blame than you deserve. Yes, you goofed up, but the other person might feel less offended if he knows your mistake wasn't an intentional slight.

This is also why you need to have considered whether there were any mitigating circumstances. It's not a good idea to make excuses when you apologize, but a simple explanation of what was going on around you when you crossed the line is not only okay, it can make your apology more credible. Let's say, for example, that you had a particularly bad bout of insomnia one night, woke up the next morning to discover that you were out of coffee and your hair dryer was on the blink, narrowly missed getting in an accident on your way to work, and arrived late for a crucial meeting. If one of your co-workers stopped by your office, breathless and fluttering, to gush about her date with the new man in her life, you'd be a stained-glass saint if you managed to refrain from blowing up at her as you threw her out of your office.

Once your meeting ended and you'd had a cup of coffee and a chance to catch your breath, however, you would probably want to seek out your colleague and apologize for having been brusque. If she's a friend as well as a co-worker, you might want to go into all the horrific details of your "morning from hell"—you could even find yourselves laughing about it together. Most of the time, however, a blow-by-blow description of all of the reasons you were rude or thoughtless is not only unnecessary, it smacks of an excuse. A simple statement—"it was a bad morning to begin with, and I was in a rush to a meeting"—is usually plenty to explain your behavior without seeming to justify it.

Then again, if the circumstances surrounding your mistake do less to excuse you and more to condemn you, you may want to handle things differently. Ask yourself whether confessing to the ugly facts will make the apology any more effective—if not, don't feel obliged to do it. Using the same example, let's say you'd had a good night's sleep, traffic was a breeze, and your meeting had been postponed, but you still blew up at your co-worker, because your own marriage was on the rocks and you just couldn't stomach her glee. Telling your infatuated colleague that you lost your temper with her because you were jealous and unhappy probably wouldn't improve your apology. It's enough to admit that you had a bad moment and tell her you're sorry.

On the other hand, if it's likely that not disclosing the full story, including your past bad behavior, will make you look like a self-serving liar when the facts emerge later, bite the bullet and tell the whole truth. To use a somewhat more serious case, let's say you got caught stealing office supplies for your kids to use at school. (It's a fairly common infraction. Many employees see this as minor pilfering at worst, but their employers, who see the total cost when all the parents in the office raid the supply cabinet every September, tend to take it a lot more seriously.) If you've truly never done it before, say so. If, however, you have been helping yourself to pens, pads, and notebooks for years, this apology might be a good time to "fess up" and wipe the slate clean. If you don't admit to what you've been doing, and the truth comes out later, you'll look a lot worse and be in a lot more trouble than you probably would have been had you been more forthcoming in the first place.

Make Amends

If you're serious about making an effective apology, you'll need to "put your money where your mouth is" and do what you must to make things right. Let's use the office supply theft as an example: Figure out how much the things you took cost your company and offer to give your boss the money back. He or she may not take it, but you will have demonstrated a willingness to pay for your mistake, which is important in an effective apology. If your boss won't take the money, donate it to a charity in your company's name. You'll be doing some good to make amends, and your apology will be more effective as a result.

Using money to make amends can be relatively painless, and that's why offering money to make amends isn't always enough. You may have to do more to make your apology stick: Spend time doing something you'd rather not do, apologize to someone else who's been injured by your conduct, or give up something that matters to you. Go ahead and do it—if you're really going to be successful in making amends, you will probably have to endure a little discomfort along the way.

You can't wipe the slate clean unless you're clear in your own mind about what you're willing to do. Revisit the section on amends in Chapter 2, and as you're thinking about how best to put things right, be creative. What will let the other person know that you're truly sorry and eager to get back on a good footing? A follow-up card or flowers or lunch at a nice restaurant? (Gifts can be a very effective way to make amends, but they carry their own risks and should not be used in place of an apology—we'll discuss that more in Chapter 5, "Choosing the Medium for Your Apology.") Perhaps spending time with that person, especially doing something the other person enjoys and you do not, would be the best way to make amends. Think of it as taking back some of the pain you caused.

In a famous fictional example, Atticus Finch, the hero of the Pulitzer Prize–winning novel *To Kill a Mockingbird*, arranged for his son, Jem, to make amends for destroying a nasty old woman's garden by reading to her every afternoon. Atticus knew (though his son did not) that old Mrs. Dubose, sick with cancer, had become addicted to painkillers and was trying to wean herself from them. Jem's reading helped her wait out the hours between doses, so that she was ultimately able to die free of her addiction. Jem hated the time he spent reading to Mrs. Dubose, but he made amends for what he had done, and in turn gave the woman a priceless gift.

The things you do to make amends will depend on the circumstances and the setting. If you're late with a report, the best way to make amends to your boss might be to do an especially good job on it when you finally turn it in. When dealing with a loved one, you're more likely to need to spend a little time, money, or attention to make things right. If you miss your daughter's softball game for the fifth time in a row due to business obligations, a few hours spent throwing a softball so she can practice batting is a small price to pay to make your apology more meaningful. Years from now, you may even find that you and your daughter look back on those hours with particular joy.

Express Appreciation

Whenever you apologize, there's at least some risk that the other person will think that you're apologizing only because you think you're obligated. Expressing appreciation for the other person lets him or her know that you're apologizing because you value your relationship, and not just because an apology is expected. This is an oft-overlooked element of a successful apology, but it's very important if you want your apology to have lasting benefits.

What you say will depend on the circumstances, but be clear about it. What do you value about the other person? Is this someone you love, respect, admire, or even treasure? Don't go beyond what you can honestly say, but don't hold back either. Too often, we neglect to tell the other people in our lives how important they are to us and how much we appreciate their presence. Especially when we hurt people, it's important to let them know how much they mean to us.

You may be worried about sounding insincere, but you can readily address that worry, and avoid sounding phony, by using simple language and not going over the top. "I really respect and admire you" is something you can say to your boss with sincerity. On the other hand, "Golly, gee whiz, you're my hero—I've never met anyone who had a greater influence on me in my entire life!" is almost certainly a bit much. Telling a casual acquaintance that she's "the most important thing in the world" to you is excessive, but that may be exactly the right thing to say to your spouse or child. If anything, be a little more appreciative than you think you should be. Many people are embarrassed by expressing strong emotion, and if you're worried about overdoing it, you're probably one of them. Push yourself a little—odds are good that you'll get it pitch perfect.

Be specific. "I really like you" is fine, but "I really value our friendship and how you're always there for me" is much better. Think back and see if you can remember a time when the other person helped you, encouraged you, stood by you, or backed you up. Thanking the other person for that support is a great way to express appreciation for his or her presence in your life.

Listen

Let the other person have his or her say when you deliver your apology. This isn't always a pleasant process, but it's essential. It's also only fair—after all, if you've hurt that person badly enough that you have to apologize, the least you can do is to let him or her talk it through.

Really try to hear what's being said. Ask questions, as needed, until you're sure you understand what the other person is telling you. People are often so busy thinking about what they're going to say next that they don't listen. If you've made the preparations discussed in Chapter 2, "Think Before You Speak," you should find it easier to stop your own internal monologue and listen to what the other person is really saying. Practice "active listening," and fully absorb the other person's words and their implications. If you sit there saying, "Uh-huh, really, yeah, I know . . . ," he or she will know you're not listening. Not only will your apology fall flat, you'll also increase the risk of reoffending him or her.

Resist the temptation to get defensive. You already know you've made a mistake, so take the feedback like a grown-up. If the wronged party thinks what you did really was that bad, who are you to say that your perspective is more accurate? You've already recognized that you need to apologize—don't compound your mistake by belittling the other person's perceptions.

By the time the person is finished, your ego may be a little bruised. It's best you get over it. If your self-image is so fragile that it crumbles at the suggestion that you might be less than perfect, it's time to give yourself a reality check. Everyone makes mistakes now and then, and the world doesn't end. Don't let your self-esteem depend on a false perception of your own infallibility. Instead, admit that you're as human as the rest of us, and feel good about the fact that you're capable of admitting to your mistakes, apologizing for them, and accepting the legitimate criticism that comes from the people you've offended.

Do Better Next Time

Resolve to behave better in the future. Of all the elements of an effective apology, this one may be the most difficult to achieve. We all have weak spots, and it's perfectly normal to make the same mistake over and over until we learn how to compensate for our weaknesses. If, for example, you tend to be forgetful, you're likely to find yourself apologizing repeatedly for missing appointments and inadvertently breaking promises. The trick is going to be learning how to change your behavior so you don't keep slipping up in the same way. You're going to get a lot more mileage out of your first apology than your tenth. If you keep repeating the same errors, people are going to doubt your sincerity, and they'll suspect (probably correctly) that you don't care about them enough to stop repeating your transgression.

One way to "do better" is to make a very specific promise about what you're going to do differently in the future, and keep it. Using bad memory as an example, let's say that you've just missed a meeting with a prospective client whose business could be worth a great deal to you and your firm. Before you call to apologize, think about what you're going to do to make sure you don't make the same mistake again. What kind of calendar do you use? If the answer is "none," go and get one. If the answer is "one that I always forget to carry with me," think about setting up your appointments on your computer or mobile phone calendar and set it to notify you whenever an appointment is pending. If you don't trust yourself to look at the notices, arrange for someone else in your office to check your calendar and nudge you if you have an appointment coming up. The point is to be creative and make a sincere effort to correct the underlying problem. Then, to make your apology truly effective, follow up with the other person and tell him or her what you have done to prevent a future offense.

*   *   *   *

Put all these elements together, and you have the makings of an effective apology. As you prepare exactly what you want to say and do when you apologize, ask yourself these questions:

- Do I sincerely want this person's forgiveness? Why? Can I clearly and honestly say that I'm sorry? Is it likely that the other person will believe me? If not, what can I do to make sure my message is understood to be sincere?

- Am I prepared to take responsibility for my mistake? Do I understand what I did wrong, and can I honestly admit it? Do I appreciate the consequences of my actions? Am I prepared to explain, but not excuse, my behavior? If there are relevant facts that really reflect badly on me, how much should I disclose?

- What should I do to make things right? How can I make amends?

- What about the other person matters most to me? Is this person a beloved spouse, cherished child, dear friend, respected colleague? Has he or she ever done something special for me, made an extra effort, or backed me up in a bad situation? How can I best express my appreciation for what this person means to me?

- What is the other person likely to say when I apologize? Am I prepared to listen? Can I accept criticism?

- How can I prevent this situation from happening again? Is there something I can do differently in the future? What does this situation tell me about myself and my relationship with the other person? What lessons do I need to learn?

When you've answered all these questions, if you're still not entirely sure what to say to the injured person, ask yourself this question: *What must I say to the other person so that I can be satisfied that I apologized as effectively as possible?*

Once you've decided what to say when you apologize, you'll need to decide when to say it. The next chapter, "Timing Your Apology," will help you do just that.

CHAPTER 4

Timing Your Apology

When you realize you've made a mistake, make amends
immediately. It's easier to eat crow while it's still warm.

—DAN HEIST

The preceding chapters have helped you gain an understanding of why you want to issue an apology, what you want the apology to accomplish, and how you can deliver the apology effectively. Now that you have decided what to say when you apologize, you need to decide when to say it. This is a very important decision, because a badly timed apology can do lasting damage. Take a few moments to consider how to pick the right time for you and for the recipient of your apology.

Find the Right Moment

It may be tempting to just go ahead and apologize to get it over with, but if that's your primary motivation, stop and think again. You may decrease your own discomfort that way, but you significantly increase the likelihood that your apology will seem perfunctory, as if you delivered it to get an inconvenient problem out of the way rather than to sincerely make things right. If your ultimate goal is to heal your relationship with the other person, wait until you've gotten yourself to the point at which you're genuinely regretful, and not just embarrassed or uncomfortable, before you apologize. Here is an example of what can go wrong if you apologize too quickly:

Lesley was a young trial attorney who was scrambling to put together documents for an emergency hearing in another city. She

33

commandeered the office copy machine, ordering Zack, the clerk who copied and collated documents for the lawyers in the firm, to put her project at the top of his to-do list. Zack was working on another important project for one of the senior partners in the firm, but Lesley, intent on her own case, neglected to ask Zack if he had other deadlines. Zack did as Lesley requested, but he felt, quite rightly, that Lesley had been inconsiderate in demanding that he drop everything to accommodate her. Barbara, the office manager, was no stranger to the temperamental ways of young attorneys; she went to Lesley and strongly suggested that Lesley apologize to Zack. Lesley did so, but she was a little embarrassed at being called on the carpet and in a hurry to get back to her hearing preparations, so she rushed through her apology, ignoring the fact that Zack made no response. Zack, not surprisingly, was doubly offended—Lesley had not only been rude in the first place, she had compounded her rudeness with a halfhearted, tossed-off apology that was blatantly insincere.

When Lesley got back from her hearing, Barbara was waiting for her. She told Lesley in no uncertain terms that her behavior toward Zack had been deplorable. Thankfully, Lesley got the message the second time around. She approached Zack respectfully, asked him when he might be available to talk to her, and apologized very sincerely for her behavior at a time that was convenient for him. Zack ultimately forgave Lesley, but it was months before they were able to work well together again. In hindsight, Lesley realized that she either should have taken the time to make a proper apology in the first place, or waited until she got back from the hearing to apologize to Zack for her original thoughtlessness.

Take Time to Calm Down

If harsh words or painful actions have been exchanged on both sides, you may decide to bite the bullet and be the first one to apologize.

That's a commendable decision, but stop and take your emotional temperature before you open your mouth. Are you still angry with the other person or upset about what was said? If so, you may want to wait a little longer, until your emotions are more contained. If you try to apologize while you're angry, you run a significant risk of losing your temper and making matters far worse. Here is an example of what can go wrong if you apologize before you have your own emotions under control:

Sydney was a character—everyone who knew him was well aware of that. He loved to regale anyone who would listen with his jokes and stories, and he never let the lateness of the hour stop him from telling just one more tale. His wife, Anne, was a quiet, soft-spoken lady who was frequently embarrassed by her husband's antics. She loved him dearly but often wished they could just go to dinner with friends or business associates without Sydney holding court for hours on end.

One night, at a business dinner with one of Anne's clients, Sydney really let loose, telling story after story and joke after joke, while Anne's client and his wife were clearly fidgeting over their cold coffee and empty dessert plates. The waiter checked in with increasing frequency to see if he could bring anything else, a sure sign that he wanted to clear the table and go home, but Sydney just kept on talking. Desperate to end the evening, Anne interrupted Sydney in the midst of yet another shaggy-dog story, saying, "Sydney, you old blowhard, that's enough. Don't you think it's time we let these nice folks go home?" She thanked their guests for a lovely evening, grabbed her coat, and practically shoved Sydney out of the restaurant.

Sydney was surprised and hurt. He thought he'd been helping Anne by charming her client and had no idea he'd gone on too long. He was offended because Anne had insulted him in front of their guests, and angry that she didn't appreciate his efforts on her behalf. Anne realized that she'd been tactless and started to apologize, but years of suppressed anger over Sydney's grandstanding suddenly erupted. Her apology quickly escalated into a full-scale explosion, and Sydney went from being mildly miffed to being absolutely devastated. It wasn't until days later that Sydney and Anne were able to begin talking to each other about what had happened, and the fight did lasting damage to their marriage. Anne realized, too late, that she should have waited until she had regained her composure to apologize to Sydney for what she originally said.

Don't Dawdle

While the preceding examples demonstrate why it can be dangerous to rush an apology, by the same token, an apology that comes too late can be worse than no apology at all. If you know that you owe someone an apology, chances are that person knows it too. Every day that you put off making the apology is another day for the other person to conclude that you don't care enough to say you're sorry. The longer you delay, the worse the other person's opinion of you is likely to become, and even if he or she ultimately forgives you, your relationship probably will never be the same. Here is an example of what can happen if you delay an apology for too long:

Richard was an ambitious young marketing executive, eager to make a reputation for himself in his new company. Don was an older marketing executive whose career with the company had reached a plateau because he was widely regarded as competent but not especially creative. Don was assigned to teach Richard the ropes as a mentor. Don was generous in giving Richard his time and attention, helping him refine his often-unfocused creative ideas and teaching the younger man everything he knew about marketing. They often talked together about how they might market particular products, with Don teaching Richard which of his ideas would work and which probably wouldn't. Due in part to Don's solid mentoring, Richard soon came to be known around the office as a real up-and-comer with a bright future.

One day the vice president for marketing asked Richard to join him for lunch. Richard was thrilled to have attracted such high-level attention, and happily answered the vice president's questions about his marketing philosophy and his ideas for how to advertise an important new product that the firm was about to launch. Richard borrowed liberally from his conversations with Don, but let the vice president think the ideas were his alone. He never said anything really bad about Don, but he didn't give him any credit for his good sense and mentoring talent, either.

Two weeks later, the vice president of marketing announced at a staff meeting that Richard would be given responsibility for conducting the advertising campaign for the new product, and provided the staff with a quick summary of what his approach would be. Don, who was no fool, recognized that Richard had taken credit for ideas that they had developed together. He said nothing at the meeting, but Richard instantly knew that Don realized what he had done.

Richard left the meeting feeling guilty and ashamed. He knew he ought to share credit for the ideas with Don, but he was reluctant to tarnish his own reputation by admitting that he had let the vice president praise him for work that wasn't entirely his and fearful that he would lose the prestigious project. He quickly became defensive, persuading himself that he had been the creative force behind the ideas and that Don really hadn't contributed all that much.

Nevertheless, Richard was honest enough to know that he owed Don an apology, but he just couldn't bring himself to do it. Days went by, then weeks, and Richard found it increasingly easier to avoid Don than to apologize. A few people in the office noticed that Richard wasn't spending much time with Don any more, but they chalked it up to his being so busy with the new project. Richard finished his marketing plan on time, and it was a huge success. Along the way, though, he lost a friend and mentor. Don left the company a few years later, and he and Richard never spoke again. When Richard looked back on the situation years later, he couldn't remember very much about the campaign, but he remembered and still deeply regretted having lost the opportunity to apologize to Don.

If You Delay, Explain

Even if you have put off an apology, you can still reverse course and make things right. You may have delayed your apology for an entirely legitimate reason. Perhaps, like Lesley, you were under time pressure and wanted to wait until you had the time to apologize properly—a very good reason for postponement. If, like Anne, you were angry, upset, or embarrassed and needed time to calm down, that's fine, too. When you finally apologize, just tell the other person why you waited. Don't make excuses for the delay—simply explain it. It's perfectly all right to say, "This is important enough that I thought I should wait until I had more time." If you were upset or angry and needed time to calm down before apologizing, you can even to say, "I wasn't sure what to say to you, and I wanted very much to get this right." If you're honest about your reasons for putting off your apology, the other person probably will forgive a short delay.

Timing an apology is all about balance. On the one hand, you need to apologize soon enough that the person you've offended will accept your apology as sincere and understand how much you value the relationship. On the other hand, you need to be sure that you have your facts straight and your emotions under control. Having an explanation at hand is therefore important if you've waited to make your apology. Each situation is different, but it's almost always right to seek a proper balance while trying to make your apology as soon as you can.

Before you make the decision about when to apologize, be sure you answer these questions:

- Have I found the right moment? Do I have the necessary time to give the other person my undivided attention? Can I avoid the temptation to take a shortcut with the apology and get on to other things?

- Do I have my emotions under control? Am I still so hurt, angry, embarrassed, or upset that I'm likely to say something I'll regret later? If not, what do I need to do to calm down enough that I can trust myself to apologize effectively?

- Have I waited to apologize? If so, why? How is the other person likely to react to the fact that I haven't apologized yet? What am I waiting for? How will I explain to the other person why I waited?

If the answers to these questions have not helped you choose the timing of your apology, ask yourself this question: *Will delaying my apology make it more effective, and if not, what am I waiting for?*

When in doubt, it's usually better to go ahead with an apology rather than to postpone it, because it's easier to clear up lingering problems with the apology than to satisfactorily explain a long delay. Lawyers like to say, "Justice delayed is justice denied." The same might be said of apologies.

CHAPTER 5

Choosing the Medium
for Your Apology

The newest computer can merely compound, at speed,
the oldest problem in the relations between human beings, and
in the end the communicator will be confronted with the
old problem, of what to say and how to say it.

—Edward R. Murrow

An important consideration in your apology, now that you have decided what to say and when to say it, is what medium to use. A face-to-face talk is usually the best way to go, as we'll discuss below. There may be, however, situations in which you simply can't make it happen. The other person may be in another city, maybe even halfway around the world. Perhaps the person you've offended won't see you. Or maybe you're so nervous about apologizing that you just can't make yourself do it in person. Luckily, you have alternatives. Depending on the circumstances, you may choose to use any of several venues or techniques.

Apologizing Face-to-Face

In most cases, apologizing in person is the most effective medium. Meeting face-to-face shows courage and sincerity on your part. You glean the added advantage of being able to see the facial expressions and body language of the person to whom you're apologizing. His or her responses can provide important cues, prompting you to adjust what you say and how you say it. Unfortunately, face-to-face can also be the scariest way to apologize, simply because there's no buffer between you and the person you have offended. You have to deal with the hurt and anger that you've caused in a very immediate way, and you usually can't just bail out once you've started. If you begin an apology in person, be prepared to see it through to the end.

Of course, that lack of a buffer is also why apologizing in person is usually the most effective approach. This is especially true if you take the opportunity to let the recipient of your apology see your genuine regret for what you did wrong and your sincere intention to make amends. An in-person meeting also requires both effort and courage on your part, and most people appreciate that. Other methods can also be effective, but if you could have apologized in person and chose not to do so, it may appear as though you took the coward's way out.

If you're going to apologize face-to-face, go to the other person— don't make him or her come to you. Make sure you've chosen a time that's convenient for that person, so you don't compound your mistake by intruding on his or her time. Allow plenty of time for the apology and the conversation that's likely to follow so you won't need to leave before you have worked things out to both parties' satisfaction.

Be sure to speak clearly and directly, and maintain good eye contact. Keep a respectful physical distance away. Don't loom in close or touch the other person unless you're absolutely certain the touch is welcome. If you're apologizing to a friend or a loved one and the discussion ends in a hug, that's fabulous, but let the other person initiate it. Don't hang back too far, though—you want to appear respectful, not reluctant.

If you're nervous about what you are going to say, practice. You may want to outline and memorize the points you intend to make and run through them several times. If you're really anxious, write out the whole apology and rehearse it like a speech in a play. Try to avoid taking notes with you, though. If your apology is so complicated that you can't remember what you plan to say unless you write it down and read it out loud, it's too complex. Try to come up with something more straightforward.

Take the time to think through what the other person is likely to say, and what your responses might be. Your apology may be just the first step in a long conversation, and you'll be better able to listen carefully if you aren't constantly distracted by thoughts of what to say next. You don't want to ruin a beautiful apology by making a careless, defensive, or tactless statement, so think about what you'll want to say, and need to avoid saying, once your apology has been delivered.

As part of your planning, before you go in to apologize, make sure you have an exit strategy. How are you going to leave once the apology has been delivered? Is there anything you absolutely have to say, or hear from the other person, before you leave the room? On the other hand, is there any topic you really need to avoid? If so, how are you going to accomplish that? Don't get too clever with this—after all, the point is to make an effective apology, not to protect yourself above all else—but recognize that a lovely apology can be spoiled by an abrupt or clumsy departure. Remind yourself of the six elements of an effective apology (Chapter 3), and take a little time to strategize so you can exit gracefully once the conversation seems to have reached the right point.

Apologizing by Phone

Apologizing on the phone can be a tricky business. Because you can't see each other's faces, you lose the benefit of being able to discern the other person's reactions, and he or she is less able to assess your sincerity. But you both can still hear each other and, to some extent, evaluate tone of voice. Using the telephone also has some advantages. A phone call is usually less formal than an in-person meeting or a letter of apology, so the telephone may be a good medium to use if you want to keep things a bit more casual. The phone also allows you to speak directly with the other person if he or she is at a physical distance, refuses to see you, or won't be available to meet with you right away when an immediate apology is called for. Additionally, if you have trouble staying on track when making an apology, the phone offers you an opportunity to talk from your notes, so you say everything you need to as you apologize.

Many of the same rules that apply when you apologize in person are also applicable to a telephone apology. Initiate the call yourself—don't make the other person call you. Make sure you've called at a convenient time, and offer to call back if the timing isn't good. Allow enough time, not just for the initial apology, but also for the discussion that will probably follow. You don't want to be distracted by another appointment or obligation while you're on the phone. Similarly, don't make the call when you're doing something else (driving, walking down the street, surfing the Internet) or in a noisy or disruptive environment. Give the recipient of your call your full attention.

Speak clearly and directly—remember, the other person can't see you. Be careful not to interrupt him or her, a particular hazard when you're talking to someone you can't see. Again, before you call, think about how the conversation is likely to go, what you need to say, what (if anything) you need to avoid saying, and how you're going to gracefully end the call. Make notes if you like—after all, no one will see them, and being able to speak from notes is one of the few real advantages of apologizing by phone. Finally, as with a face-to-face apology, practice as necessary until you're ready to call.

What if you get voice mail or an answering machine? Should you leave a message? That, of course, depends on the situation. If your transgression was pretty minor, leave a message that you called to apologize and promise to call back. Be sure to follow up on that promise—your initial message won't count as a real apology, and failing to call when you've promised to do so will only compound your mistake.

If, on the other hand, you've done something seriously wrong, leave a message that you've called and would like to talk, but don't get into the specifics. There will be time for that when you finally connect. Keep calling until you get through, but don't leave a message every time. Your goal is to apologize, not to demonstrate how hard you're trying to do so, and the other person may take multiple messages from you as a not-so-subtle criticism that he or she should have been easier to reach.

Apologizing in a Letter

Written apologies have certain advantages. They allow you to think carefully about what you want to say, and to write and rewrite until you have exactly the right message. They let you deliver your initial message without any unpleasant confrontation or the need to plan an exit strategy. They give the recipient an opportunity to cool off before responding to what you've had to say. There's also a lovely, old-fashioned formality to a written letter of apology that can strike just the right tone, especially in a business setting.

On the other hand, a written apology can be easily misunderstood. The other person can't hear the tone of your voice or see your facial expressions, so he or she will interpret the words you write in his or her voice, not yours. If you use a badly chosen phrase or leave something out, the other person is likely to notice, and may take additional offense. Remember, he or she is already angry, hurt, or otherwise upset, or you wouldn't be apologizing in the first place. An affronted person isn't likely to read your words as charitably as he or she otherwise might have, given the circumstances, and may be angry enough to actually look for reasons to get even more offended by what you've written. A written apology may also fall flat if you could easily have apologized in person. The recipient may decide that you were too cowardly, or not sufficiently concerned with mending fences, to bite the bullet and apologize face-to-face. (If he or she would be right about that, scrap the written apology and schedule a meeting.)

If you do choose to apologize in writing, your letter needn't be pages long—a simple note may be enough, depending on the circumstances. In most instances, shorter is probably better, because it gives you less opportunity for overly elaborate explanations that can read like excuses. Don't use words you don't understand, and check your spelling. An apology letter full of misused language and spelling mistakes will seem careless—and possibly uncaring. Take the time to do a quality job. One important caveat: While typed letters are fine in many circumstances, in a personal relationship, it's best if you skip the keyboard and handwrite a letter on nice stationery. Even if your handwriting wouldn't win any awards, a typed letter is too impersonal for saying "I'm sorry" to someone you love.

If the other person won't talk to you, or is miles away, or if something more formal than a simple "I'm sorry" is needed, a letter of apology may be the way to go. You won't have an immediate opportunity to discuss your apology with the other person, so it's important for your letter to be as complete as possible. Before you sign, stamp, and send it, go back over the six essential elements of an apology (Chapter 3) and make sure your letter covers all the basics. Some of the elements—in particular, listening while the other person has her say—will not fit readily into a letter. You may want to add that you'll follow up with a phone call, so the two of you can talk together about what happened.

Apologizing by Email

Although email makes communication easier and more efficient in myriad ways, an emailed apology is a disaster waiting to happen. Even the best-written email tends to look extremely casual, and people who write email on a regular basis frequently get sloppy about spelling, grammar, and word choice. An emailed apology will almost certainly strike the other person as slapdash and insincere. If you have any choice at all, do not apologize by email.

One possible exception is if you're in the unfortunate position of having to apologize to a great many people very quickly. Let's say, for example, that you invited thousands of your company's shareholders to a meeting and got the date wrong on the invitation. Let's suppose further that the only way to get word of your mistake to all of those people in time would be to use email. In an instance like that, an email apology might be appropriate, but a follow-up letter of apology would probably also be a very good idea.

Apologizing with a Greeting Card, E-card, or App

Stationery shops and websites are chock-full of ready-made cards with apologies written by someone else. Electronic apology cards abound on all the major e-card sites. Many of them are well done, but they all have the same drawbacks: They were written for use by lots of people in a wide variety of situations, so they tend to be fairly generic; and they weren't written by you, so they're less personal than a letter or note that you wrote yourself would be.

Recognize, too, that the person you're apologizing to may not appreciate receiving a preprinted apology. Some people think of greeting cards as little gifts, and might see an apology card as a lovely peace offering. Others see greeting cards as a lazy alternative to a personal expression of regret. Unless you're sure that the person to whom you owe an apology will welcome it in a greeting card, write a letter or apologize in person or on the phone.

If you're going to use an apology card, unless it says exactly what you would have said if you'd written a letter of apology, and says it better than you ever possibly could, you need to augment its message. Use the card, but add a handwritten (or, in the case of an e-card, typed) note that refers to your specific situation and expresses your regrets in your own words. Again, review the six elements of an effective apology (Chapter 3), and make sure that within the preprinted text and your own note, you've covered everything you need to say. A few extra words from you will vastly increase the likelihood that the apology in the card you send will be effective.

These days there seems to be an "app" for everything, and indeed there are apps for smartphones and tablet computers that provide a selection of ready-made apologies. One app even allows the sender to choose the tone of apology on a scale ranging from "heartfelt" to "funny." These apps aren't all bad, but they suffer from the same impersonality as apology cards, and have the added disadvantage of being so easy to send that they can seem thoughtless. They're also often intended to be funny, which means they can be insulting to an already-injured person who isn't in the mood to joke. Unless you're absolutely sure that the person receiving your apology won't be offended by receiving a short, canned electronic apology, pick another medium.

Apologizing in an Online Forum

There are a multitude of public forums for apologies. An apology can be posted on someone's Facebook wall, tweeted and retweeted around the world, recorded on YouTube, embedded in a blog post, splashed across any of several apology websites, or even artistically arranged on a content-sharing forum such as Pinterest. Such public apologies can be very effective when one is dealing with crowds. For example, a manufacturer that wants to apologize to all of its customers for a product recall can do so on its company blog (see Chapter 10, "Public Apologies," for ways to handle that situation).

You may want to consider posting a public apology if you offended someone in a public setting. Let's say, for example, that you insulted your child's teacher at a parent-teacher association meeting, and everyone in attendance heard you. Apologizing to the teacher in a private meeting may not be enough to wipe the slate clean. Following up the face-to-face meeting with a posted apology on the PTA website's chat room or other forum might help assuage the teacher's hurt feelings and clear up any lingering concerns among the other people who overheard you.

If you need to make an apology to an individual, however, think carefully before doing it in a public online setting. If your actions were sufficiently embarrassing or hurtful to her, she may not want the incident to be brought up in public again. Using the example in the previous paragraph, your child's teacher might prefer not to have your criticisms of her aired in public for a second time, so get her permission before making a public post. Sending a separate note to the principal praising your child's teacher might be a better way to make amends than posting something online.

Apologizing with a Gift

Many people think that giving a gift—flowers, chocolate, jewelry, wine—is a great way to apologize. In some instances they may be right, but using a gift as an apology has certain risks attached.

It's very important that an apology gift be appropriate to the circumstances. Flowers can be lovely, but they can also send the wrong message, especially between a man and a woman or a supervisor and a staffer. (An example of a gift of flowers between a male and female colleague flopping spectacularly is described in the section "The hazards of gift giving" in Chapter 6, "Apologies in the Workplace.") Unless the recipient is your sweetheart or spouse, or is someone with whom it's very clear you are not pursuing a romantic relationship, flowers are generally not a good apology gift. The same goes for jewelry, candy, and any other gift that lovers routinely exchange. In any platonic relationship, avoid sending a gift that smacks of romance.

It's critical that the gift not appear in any way to be a bribe. If you've hurt or offended someone, offering a gift (especially an expensive one) can give the appearance that you're trying to buy his or her forgiveness. Even if the person accepts the gift, he or she is likely to wonder later whether you were really sorry or if you just bought the gift so you wouldn't have to actually admit that you'd made a mistake.

As with any form of apology, an apology gift might work once, twice, or even three times, but eventually the other person is going to get tired of your behavior. The philandering husband who shows up with roses for his wife every time he starts a new affair may be a laughable cliché on television, but in the real world, injuring the same person over and over, and trying to smooth the hurt over with a gift, is atrocious behavior. A gift may earn you forgiveness occasionally, but don't expect gifts to make up for your misdeeds forever.

That said, gifts do have their place in apologies, and they can be useful as part of an effective apology when it comes to making amends. If, for example, you broke an expensive wineglass at a friend's dinner party, replacing the glass would be an appropriate and undoubtedly appreciated part of your apology. If you want to give a gift, though, don't feel you have to limit yourself to physical objects. You can also give your time, your attention, and other resources. Suppose, for example, you keep your administrative assistant long after hours one evening because you are late with a project that needed to be collated and copied; order in some dinner for him, or offer to let him go home early Friday afternoon. If you missed your daughter's ballet recital because you were caught in traffic, spend an extra half hour with her and watch her repeat her performance in the living room. A gift that helps correct your offense is one that is most likely to make your apology effective.

As you're weighing the best medium for your apology, be sure you have asked yourself, and answered, these questions:

- Should I apologize in person, on the phone, or some other way? If I'm not going to apologize in person, what are my reasons for picking another medium?

- If I'm apologizing in person, what will I need to say? What, if anything, do I need to leave out? Should I prepare notes? Will practicing before I apologize make my apology more effective? How will I gracefully end the conversation once my apology has been delivered?

- If I'm apologizing by telephone, what should I be sure to say? Will I be more effective with notes in front of me? Should I practice first so my apology will be more effective? How will I gracefully get off the phone after apologizing? If no one answers, should I leave a message?

- If I'm going to send a letter of apology, what should I write in it? What do I need to do to ensure that my spelling and grammar are correct? Should I ask someone else to read it to be sure I haven't accidentally said something that might offend the recipient? How will I make sure that the person receiving my apology has a chance to tell me how my actions affected him?

- If I'm going to use a preprinted card or an e-card, what should I write to supplement the generic text? Is there anything I should do to follow up and make my apology more effective? If I want to use an apology app, am I sure the other person won't be offended by it? What can I do to make the apology more personal?

- If I'm going to post my apology online, do I need to restrict access somehow, so the recipient won't be embarrassed or offended? If I'm posting my apology to reach a large group of people, will I need to do anything else to apologize to people who won't necessarily see it?

- Should I include a gift as part of my apology? Will the other person appreciate receiving a gift, or will it look like a bribe? If I'm going to give a gift, what should it be?

If the answers to these questions haven't helped you decide what medium to use when you apologize, ask yourself this: *Even if it makes me uncomfortable, what medium is most likely to make my apology as effective as possible, and if I'm not willing to use that medium, why not?*

Answer that question, and you'll be ready to decide which medium to use. And now that we've examined the fundamentals of the art of the apology, it's time to turn to specifics. The next several chapters address how to apologize in various settings and to particular kinds of people. They'll help you tailor your apology to best address your individual situation.

PART TWO

THE APOLOGY

CHAPTER 6

Apologies in the Workplace

A day of worry is more exhausting than a day of work.
—JOHN LUBBOCK

If you work an average of forty hours a week, you probably spend more of your waking hours at your company and with your co-workers than you do at home with your family and friends. Good relationships in your workplace are essential to your company's overall success, as well as to your professional future, influencing your opportunities to garner raises, promotions, and plum projects, and your job security. Conversely, a transgression, such as a bad blowup with your boss, a colleague, or even a support staffer, can severely damage your professional future.

The Special Circumstances of the Workplace

Workplace apologies, like all others, should still include the six essential elements outlined in Chapter 3. Additionally, the office comes with particular conditions that might become pitfalls if you don't take them into account. We'll go into those before we get to the fine points of workplace apologies themselves.

Office politics. Navigating the emotional waters of the workplace, unfortunately, can often be filled with peril. While it would be wonderful if everyone always got along at work, the truth is that personalities clash, egos take over, and office politics can be a constant hazard. The old adage "You can choose your friends, but you can't choose your relatives" goes double for your co-workers. Even if you are fortunate enough to find a great boss and fabulous colleagues, conflicts among you can still arise. Turnover can change even the best office environment over time, as less congenial personalities may replace professional friends, or newcomers simply begin to influence the way things are done. If you want to succeed in your job, you have to be able to get along reasonably well with just about everyone, and being able to apologize effectively can be an essential weapon in your professional arsenal.

Apologizing in a politically fraught office can seem so hazardous that even when you know you've made a mistake, you may be tempted to just hunker down and hope things will blow over rather than admit that you were wrong. Resist that temptation. Being able to apologize effectively is a tremendous skill in any workplace, and demonstrates confidence and maturity. The ability to apologize can help you survive even in a highly politicized work setting and, if you're in a position to do so and willing to invest the time and effort, can even help you set a more accepting, collaborative tone that will benefit everyone in your office.

The hazards of gift giving. Offering a gift as part of an apology can be a good way to make amends in private relationships, but selecting an appropriate gift can be particularly risky in the workplace. Your company may have rules about what gifts employees can accept from each other, and you don't want to compound your mistake by encouraging a person you have offended to violate company policy. Perhaps more important, though, a gift to a co-worker can convey the wrong message, especially if the gift seems like a bribe or sends the wrong signal about what you think of the other person. Giving a gift to a superior can look as if you're trying to buy your way out of trouble—never a good idea—and giving a gift to a peer or a member of the support staff can seem condescending. Here's an example of an apology gift that was a spectacular failure:

James and Clara were department heads of a nonprofit membership association. James, an ambitious man, was eager to take over the newly vacant executive director's position. Clara had been with the association for many years; gregarious and personable, she was a favorite with the members. James recognized Clara's popularity and realized that she could help him tremendously with the organization's members and, in particular, the search committee. Still, James resented the influence Clara's popularity gave her, since he privately thought of her as an intellectual lightweight who got by on charm rather than hard work and talent. One day James lost his temper with Clara, shouting at her over what he instantly realized had been, at worst, a minor transgression on her part. Clara fled to her office, and James knew that he had made a serious tactical error. He immediately went to a nearby florist and purchased an elaborate bouquet of flowers, which he presented to Clara with an equally florid apology.

Clara took the flowers and accepted James's apology in the heat of the moment, but she became less enchanted with both the more she thought back on what James had done. Clara was well aware that James didn't think much of her talents or her popularity with the members of their association. She guessed that his apology was motivated not by a desire to mend fences but to get her support for his candidacy for the executive director position. Clara was also sure that James would never have given flowers to a man. The gift began to seem like a bribe, and a sexist, demeaning bribe at that. Clara didn't go out of her way to make trouble for James, but she did nothing to help him with his candidacy, either. The search committee ultimately selected another candidate for the executive director position, and James, disappointed, left the association soon thereafter.

If you feel compelled to give a gift to a co-worker as a way of making amends, it's usually preferable to keep the gift financially modest and gender-neutral. For example, taking the other person to lunch or out for a drink after work might be effective. Most often, however, the best gift you can give is your time and effort. Help your colleague finish a project, back her up in a public meeting, or drop your boss a memo or email describing something your co-worker said or did that you thought was particularly terrific. Helping your colleague shine in the workplace is a great way to make your apology effective and to strengthen your relationship in the future.

The company hierarchy. The people who work in a company can be categorized in a variety of ways. For our purposes, we'll use the company's organizational chart as a rough indicator of company hierarchy. (Apologizing to customers and clients is a separate matter that is addressed in the next chapter, "Apologizing in Business.") Your co-workers usually fall into three broad categories: superiors (your immediate supervisor and those to whom she reports, as well as anyone else who's above you on the organizational chart), your peers (people who are approximately on your level in the company), and people ranked beneath you on the company's organizational chart, whether they report to you or not. Within each category there are, of course, variations—the president's administrative assistant typically commands considerably more deference than the general receptionist, even if they're both at the same level on the organizational chart—but the applicable principles are essentially the same. While the six elements of an effective apology are as essential to a workplace apology as they are in any other setting, other elements shift in the workplace depending on whether you're apologizing to a superior, a peer, or someone whose rank falls beneath yours.

Apologizing to Superiors

If you have to apologize to one or more people in your company who are superior to you in rank, there are a few essential principles to keep in mind as you develop and deliver your apology.

Talk to your boss first. If you need to issue an apology to someone superior to you in the hierarchy, make sure to tell your boss what has happened (unless, of course, you're apologizing to your boss), preferably before you apologize. There are several good reasons to do this. If you and your boss have a good relationship, she may be able to help you in making your apology effective, and she can assist you in managing any fallout. If you're nervous about apologizing to the other person, it might be a good idea to have your boss arrange the meeting and sit in. Even if you don't have the world's best relationship with your boss, it's important to let her know what happened. Otherwise, she may be taken by surprise when your actions are revealed, and very few bosses appreciate nasty surprises. If you don't come clean with your boss before you apologize to the higher-up, you'll almost certainly end up having to apologize separately to her, not only for whatever you did in the first place but also for failing to keep her in the loop.

Use deference. The further up the company hierarchy you go, the more likely it is that the person to whom you're apologizing is accustomed to being treated with a great deal of respect. It's not a good idea to be disrespectful to a superior in the middle of an apology. This is especially important if the mistake you're apologizing for involved being rude or insubordinate with that superior. Do not, under any circumstances, compound the problem by delivering a less than respectful apology. Be extremely courteous as you apologize, and be very careful to avoid seeming defensive or hostile. And avoid making jokes—they'll rarely be seen as funny.

If, on the other hand, you haven't been disrespectful or insubordinate, you can probably afford to relax, but just a little. You still want to be appropriately deferential, but since your actions and not your attitude are at issue, there shouldn't be a need to grovel. Be straightforward and polite, stick to the facts, and don't dramatize or exaggerate your remorse.

Don't interrupt. Once you've made your apology, your superior gets the floor for as long as he or she wants it. If your superior makes a factual mistake when responding to your apology, wait until he or she has clearly finished speaking before you politely correct it. Let's say, for example, that you accidentally overstated quarterly sales by five percent in a report to your company's president, and you've notified your boss and apologized. If your boss, while thinking out loud about how to correct your error without losing the president's confidence, makes reference to a fifteen percent overstatement, wait until he has finished speaking before correcting the mistake. Interrupting will only make you seem defensive.

Tell the whole truth. If you've made a serious mistake, tell your superiors everything at once. It may be tempting to disclose only the bare minimum, but don't make that error. Get everything out in the open. Otherwise, you'll end up looking foolish at best and dishonest at worst when the whole ugly truth comes out later. (And make no mistake about it—sooner or later, the truth will come out.) Here's an example of what can happen if you tell only part of the truth to your superiors when making an apology:

Ted was the executive director of a not-for-profit community service organization. Although he had worked in community service for many years, his prior assignments had focused on individual counseling and community outreach; he had never been required to manage a budget, oversee a staff, or produce a monthly newsletter. Ted had difficulty juggling his new responsibilities and found it particularly difficult to write his monthly newsletters. He started cutting and pasting other writers' work without attribution. Unfortunately for Ted, one of his volunteers recognized one of the pieces he had lifted, and reported Ted's plagiarism to the chair of the organization's volunteer board of directors.

When confronted by the board, Ted admitted that he had plagiarized other writers' work, but admitted to only a few instances of having done so. One of the board members did some independent research, however, and quickly discovered more than two dozen examples of plagiarism in Ted's writing, including the sample piece he submitted to get the job. The board fired Ted, not so much for the plagiarism as for failing to make full disclosure when he was first questioned. Ted not only lost his job, he lost his good reputation in the not-for-profit community, and his future opportunities for public service were severely limited.

Offer a solution. In a business setting, part of making amends is being ready with a workable solution. Before you apologize, make sure you've thought through the implications of what you did wrong and come up with a practical way to solve the problem you've created. This has two advantages. First, it shows your superiors that you understand what you've done wrong and have put effort into considering how to fix it. Second, it gives you something positive to focus on, which will calm your nerves and help you apologize in a more professional way. For example, suppose you prepared a first draft of a report to a client, and your boss made significant corrections to your draft. In the process of getting the report out the door, you accidentally sent your first draft to the client instead of the version containing your boss's edits. When apologizing to your boss, come prepared with a strategy for how to tell the client about the mistake. Even if your boss doesn't use your idea, he or she will appreciate the effort you made to help mend fences with the client.

Repeat your story as necessary. The bigger your mistake was, the more often you will have to tell your story. You may have cost your company money, created an accounting problem, seriously damaged a relationship with a client or customer, or even exposed your company to a lawsuit. If your mistake was serious enough to cause potential harm to your company's long-term interests, be prepared to have other people—your boss's boss, the company's accountants, the company's attorney, the public relations team, and others—brought in to talk with you about what you did and how you did it. Don't get defensive. If you've created a problem for your company, their expert help may be just the thing needed to fix it. Relax, tell your full story, and recognize that cooperation and courtesy on your part will go a long way toward restoring your good reputation. Here's an example of a situation in which one employee did just that:

Jean-Luc was a young financial analyst with a company that provided consulting services on corporate mergers and acquisitions. His job was to estimate the value of the assets and liabilities of companies for sale, so that buyers would know how much to offer for them. Jean-Luc's job was stressful, requiring fast, accurate work, long hours, and late nights. One evening, while working late after little sleep, Jean-Luc made a serious mathematical error as part of a series of complex calculations. He wrongly concluded that Sellco, a company for sale, was worth millions of dollars more than it actually was. His firm reported Jean-Luc's estimate to its client company, Buyer, Inc., which purchased Sellco based in part on the strength of Jean-Luc's estimate.

It was not until after the acquisition was complete that Jean-Luc realized that he had overvalued Sellco by approximately ten million dollars. After a sleepless night, Jean-Luc went to his boss, admitted what he had done, and apologized for the error. That conversation began a seemingly endless round of discussions with the management of his firm, the attorneys, and other analysts, as the firm's management decided how best to manage the error. Jean-Luc was patient, apologetic, and straightforward in all of the meetings, even though he was embarrassed by what he had done and occasionally frustrated by having to tell his story again and again. Ultimately, the president of Jean-Luc's firm notified Buyer, Inc., of the error, and negotiated a deal with Buyer, Inc., to resolve the matter. Jean-Luc expected to find that the incident left a black mark on his record, but was delighted at year-end to receive a solid work review and a handsome raise. His superiors had appreciated his honesty in coming forward and his stalwart, patient behavior through the process of resolving the problem.

Apologizing to Peers

Apologizing to a peer may seem easier than making an apology to a superior, but that isn't always the case. Peer relationships can get complicated, and it's important to be as careful with people at or about your level in your company as you are with your bosses. If you have to apologize to one of your peers, there are a few essential principles to keep in mind as you develop and deliver your apology.

K.I.S.S.: *Keep It Simple, Sarah (or Sam).* When you apologize to a peer at work, it's usually not a great tactic to offer an elaborate explanation for what you did wrong. If you're on good terms with your colleague, a blow-by-blow "mea culpa" shouldn't be necessary, and if you're not, dwelling on the details may make your mistake seem like a bigger deal than it is. State the relevant facts, but don't feel obliged to say more than you really must to take appropriate responsibility for your actions. Unless you're dealing with a personal friend who happens to work where you do (in that case, read Chapter 8, "Apologizing to Loved Ones"), a brief, matter-of-fact summary of what happened should suffice.

Prepare for politics. If you've offended someone who likes to play office politics, recognize that fact and deal with it before you make your apology. Don't use the other person's propensity to play games as an excuse to avoid apologizing—he or she will simply use your failure to apologize against you, characterizing you as rude, uncooperative, or otherwise. Just recognize that your colleague may try to use your apology to his or her advantage, and talk to whomever else you need to either before or just after you apologize. If, for example, you lost your temper with the office manager and you know he'll complain to his boss, the chief operating officer, tell your boss what happened and confirm that you're planning to apologize. This allows your boss to be prepared to run interference if the COO decides to make your behavior an issue. You may also want to talk to the COO yourself, explaining your side of the story and apologizing for having upset her employee.

Apologizing to Lower-Ranking Colleagues

Depending on where you are in the company hierarchy, there are probably people who show up below you on the office organizational chart. These employees are often the backbone of an organization, doing important work to keep the company going. If you find yourself having to apologize to a member of the support staff, or someone otherwise subordinate to you, there are a few principles to keep in mind.

Swallow your pride. If you're concerned that your peers and superiors may lose respect for you if you apologize to a member of the support staff, put that notion aside. An effective apology to a subordinate worker builds lasting loyalty and can help you develop and maintain a great reputation in your workplace. By contrast, withholding apologies from support staff who deserve them so you can look like a tough guy or because you feel superior to them can backfire, leaving you with a bad reputation and a world of trouble getting things done. Here's an example of what happened to one person who let concerns for his image prevent him from making apologies:

Curt was a retired Air Force officer who went to work for a financial services company. Brash and outspoken, Curt had a hard-nosed approach to hierarchy, and he wasn't shy about dressing down anyone in the office whose work he considered to be substandard, whether those people reported to him or not. He thought it was important to project the image of a tough guy, and went out of his way to do so. Within a few months, he had alienated the mail clerk, the receptionist, the computer support staff, and every administrative assistant in the office. Soon, Curt's mail was being delivered late if at all, his phone messages got "lost," his important client files were conveniently "misplaced," his documents disappeared from the copy machine, and he found himself waiting hours or even days for computer technical support. As Curt grew more frustrated and outspoken, the service he received in the office got worse.

Finally, one of his peers took pity on Curt, took him to lunch, and told him what was happening, explaining that he couldn't treat his civilian subordinates in the office the way he had his enlisted troops. It took Curt a few days to come to terms with what his colleague had said, but eventually he recognized that his attitude toward those who worked for him needed adjusting. He began treating them with greater respect, apologizing sincerely when he forgot and slipped back into his old bullying ways. Over time, Curt's relations in the office improved, and he was able to serve his financial clients far more effectively.

Make kindness key. The fact that someone is below you in the office hierarchy is no reason to treat him or her disrespectfully. If anything, it's a reason to be particularly considerate and sincere when you apologize. A person with less leverage in the workplace may not be in a position to tell you off if you say or do something hurtful or offensive, but that doesn't mean he or she doesn't resent what you did or deserve the best apology you can offer. You're both working to make the com-

pany a success and, although the person's work may seem less important to you than your own, your company could suffer serious
problems if it didn't get done well and on time. Be as polite when you
apologize to a subordinate staffer as you would be when talking to the
president of your company; your apology is much more likely to be
effective.

Don't apologize in private if you erred in public. Although this
principle applies to any apology, it's particularly important when
you're apologizing to someone below you in the company hierarchy.
Remember, the support staffer, who probably isn't in a position to
challenge you if you say or do something offensive in public, is every
bit as concerned about his or her good reputation as you are about
yours. If, for example, you blamed a clerical error on your boss's
administrative assistant in front of your boss, then apologized privately to the assistant later, you won't have done anything to help him
recover in the boss's eyes. You can bet the administrative assistant
knows that, too, and will harbor a grudge if you don't make things
right. Make sure your boss hears the apology, too, or it probably won't
be effective.

Report your actions as necessary. If you've offended a member of the
support staff who reports to one of your peers, consider whether you
should also talk to your peer and your boss about what happened.
Even if you've apologized to the employee, there may still be bad feeling that could poison your work environment, especially if your peer
or boss decides that you tried to sweep the matter under the rug. It
may be embarrassing to admit that you made an inappropriate joke to
the receptionist or lost your temper with the mail clerk, but in most
instances, confessing to what you did and letting your peer or boss
know you've made a full apology is usually far better than having
them hear about the incident through the company grapevine.

After You Apologize

There are two other things you may want to do after you have delivered a workplace apology. Ideally, your actions should serve to both smooth relations with your colleague and protect you if the situation somehow turns nasty again.

Document the outcome. Once you've made your apology and it has been accepted, it's often a good idea to make a record of what happened. Documenting the outcome can have several benefits. It confirms that the conversation took place, demonstrates your belief that things have been set to rights, and proves that you did the right thing by apologizing to the other person. It also gives you an opportunity to confirm the next steps you've agreed to take, so that any misunderstandings can be ironed out before they become major problems.

Even after a relatively minor infraction, you may want to drop a short memo or email to the person who received your apology, expressing your thanks for the conversation and confirming what you've agreed to do to make amends. For example, suppose one of your colleagues made a less-than-brilliant suggestion when you two were about to go give a presentation in a staff meeting, and you condescendingly dismissed it. After the meeting, realizing you had been rude, you apologized to your colleague, and you suggested you meet the next day to talk about the idea you had dismissed. Though still a little miffed, your colleague accepted your apology and your offer. A quick email—"Thanks for talking to me this afternoon; just wanted to say again that I'm sorry I was impolite to you before this morning's meeting. I look forward to hearing more about your idea tomorrow"—might be a smart way to follow up on your initial apology. Although email is usually a terrible medium for making apologies, it can be a great tool to document the fact that you apologized and promised to make things right.

Follow through as usual. Ultimately, workplace apologies aren't terribly different from apologies in other settings. Make sure you follow up on your promises to make amends, documenting their completion with a memo or email to the injured party, and circle back as necessary to confirm that you've cleaned the slate with your colleague.

*   *   *   *

If you apologize effectively to your co-workers, you will begin to build and maintain a solid reputation in your company. Learning to apologize effectively to clients and customers, likewise, can help you build a solid business. That's next.

CHAPTER 7

Apologizing in Business

(and Why Your Lawyer May Object!)

The good lawyer is not the man who has an eye to
every side and angle of contingency, and qualifies all his
qualifications, but who throws himself on your part
so heartily, that he can get you out of a scrape.

—RALPH WALDO EMERSON

Just as it's important to be able to apologize successfully to the people you see from day to day in your workplace, it's absolutely critical to be able to apologize effectively to the clients and customers who purchase your company's goods and services. No matter how hard and carefully you and everyone in your company work, things simply are going go wrong from time to time. Quality controls fail, accidents happen, mistakes get made, judgments prove to be faulty—it's all part of life. Until people become perfect, it's an unfortunate but inescapable fact that apologies to clients and customers are going to be in order now and then.

Unfortunately, it seems to be a driving myth of American society that nothing should ever go wrong and, if it does, a scapegoat must be identified immediately and severely punished. Just watch any widely publicized tragedy, from a plane crash to a hurricane. Inevitably, after the first shock of the crisis is over, the finger-pointing starts, the lawsuits get filed, the press fans the flames, and the people who tried to prevent or manage the tragedy often find themselves scrambling to avoid having their lives, careers, and reputations destroyed. There has to be a better way.

In this chapter, we'll focus on business apologies; we'll cover general business mistakes, individual customer service slipups, and professional malpractice. And because litigation is a way of life in corporate America, we'll address the impact that apologies can have when businesses go to court.

Addressing Business Mistakes

Businesses strive to develop and maintain good relations with their clients and customers, but those relationships usually aren't as personal as those among friends, families, and even co-workers. On one hand, that can be good, because it usually prevents clients and customers from taking a business mistake as a personal betrayal. On the other hand, clients and customers usually don't have as much emotionally invested in business relationships, so they're more likely to walk away if something goes wrong and a business fails to make an effective apology. The same can be true of contractors and suppliers, who may see your company as an unreliable partner if mistakes aren't addressed with effective apologies.

Even in the best of economic times, no business can afford to fritter away customers or jeopardize good relations with a client. The six elements of an effective apology (Chapter 3) are as important in business relationships as they are in personal ones. Here are some highlights on how they apply in various business settings.

General business errors. Whether your company has made a miscalculation of how long it will take to deliver a product, underestimated the costs of a job, or discovered a flaw in a product after it has gone out the door, it's a mistake to leave a problem unresolved. For example, let's say that your company was hired to purchase and install flooring throughout a large new hotel. The team that measured the space made a mathematical error and ordered too much hardwood and not enough carpet. To make matters worse, the carpet your client selected was end-of-run, and you can't get any more. Here are some steps to keep in mind when preparing to apologize to your customer:

Do your homework. Before you simply say the carpet is unavailable, look into alternative sources. Maybe your supplier has run out of carpet, but it's possible that another supplier has more or that the manufacturer still has some in stock. If you can find more, buy it for any rational price. After all, the mistake was yours, and it's worth spending a little extra money to maintain your company's good reputation. If there's really no more to be had, get samples of complementary alternatives (be sure they're large enough to allow your customer to make a meaningful choice) and have them in hand before speaking with your customer.

Come up with a bonus. If you can't provide the carpet your client ordered, maybe you can offer to provide another design element that will complement the alternative carpet samples you've collected. There may be wallpaper, light fixtures, or a paint treatment that would make the alternatives look even better than the original choice. If you're not confident of satisfying your customer's taste, consider offering to pay an interior designer of his or her choice to develop a new design scheme to go with inventory you know you can get.

Take action, the sooner, the better. Problems rarely improve when neglected, and that's particularly true in a business setting. Especially if your customer is facing a deadline (perhaps the new hotel is scheduled to open just in time for summer vacations), you'll need to make your apology as quickly as you can. There's no sense in compounding the problem by dragging your feet.

Customer service snafus. When you think about it, most consumers ask relatively little of the companies who sell them products and services, but the things they do expect can be deal breakers if your company doesn't deliver. For example, customers expect merchandise to be of good quality, to hold up to normal use, and to meet regulatory requirements and industry standards, especially where their physical safety is concerned. They expect salespeople to be courteous, service to be reasonably timely, and returns to be accepted within reasonable limits. They generally expect to be warned of known hazards and pitfalls, especially if companies think those hazards are likely to become a problem.

The good news is that your customers know you're only human and typically don't expect perfection—unless you promise it to them. In the highly competitive American marketplace, it can be tempting to promise more than you and your company can deliver. If you do that, you practically guarantee that you'll disappoint your customers or clients sooner or later, and apologies will be owed. If, for example, your restaurant promises lunchtime diners that they'll be "in and out in thirty minutes," and your servers routinely fail to meet that goal, your restaurant will likely lose customers. Yes, you can apologize, but if you merely say you're sorry every day for the same mishap, you'll be lucky if your customers wait around long enough to roll their eyes before they leave your premises.

When something goes wrong, customers also expect prompt notice and an honest and complete explanation. They're not interested in having bad news dished out to them in bite-size pieces—they want the truth, and they want it all at once. Holding back bad news is a great way to damage customer trust, especially if your customers think you've been running a cover-up. Every business-school student knows that, but for some reason American companies seem particularly reluctant to admit to the amount of trouble a problem is likely to cause. Airlines, for one example, often seem to understate the length of time involved in weather delays or equipment failures. It may be that their estimates are honest, though perhaps too optimistic, but travelers frequently complain that airlines simply lie.

No matter how big and successful your company may be, an unhappy customer can cause you a world of trouble. That's especially true in the Internet age, now that a disgruntled consumer can instantly blast his discontent around the globe. If you're in the difficult position of having to apologize to an angry customer for a service snafu, here are some things to keep in mind:

Keep it human. Give your disappointed customer a real person, with a name, face, and phone number, to help resolve her complaint. Don't make her run the gauntlet of an automated telephone or email system to get help—make sure a well-trained, courteous, responsive human representative of your company is available in person or on the phone. Additionally, be sure your company's representative has the authority to take reasonable steps to make amends. If, for example, a customer purchased an expensive piece of crystal from your company and it arrived broken, make sure your customer service representative is authorized to replace the item on the spot without going up the company ladder for permission.

Unfortunately, too many companies fail to give their employees sufficient discretion to mollify unhappy customers. Here's an example of how one unhappy shopper reacted to an inflexible corporate stance:

Lucy had purchased an inexpensive cocktail shaker from a megastore's online operation to be part of a gift basket for a friend. The shaker arrived too late to be included in the basket, so Lucy decided to return the shaker when it finally arrived. She took it to a local branch of the megastore, only to discover that the store would only accept the return by mail. Lucy was annoyed—the cost of shipping would be almost half the cost of the shaker, and she didn't understand why the store refused to accept a timely return of its own merchandise. The customer service manager politely told Lucy that he was sorry she was unhappy—in fact, he told her that repeatedly in response to every argument Lucy made. Eventually he suggested that she file a complaint with "Corporate," an invitation that Lucy took as proof that any further objection on her part would simply vanish into the store's vast and complicated internal structure. She left the store angry and frustrated, returned the shaker by mail, and never patronized the store again.

The loss of Lucy's business was, no doubt, of little concern to a gigantic company with millions of customers. Lucy herself recognized that the matter was trivial, but remained annoyed with how the customer service manager had stonewalled her. A sincere apology on the part of the customer service manager would have gone a long way toward making Lucy into a loyal customer. As it was, Lucy not only refused to return to the store, she made sure that her many Facebook friends knew the story, too.

Avoid "corporatespeak." There are certain phrases that businesses commonly use when they want to pay lip service to their customers but don't want to admit they've done anything wrong. "We regret any inconvenience" is one example. It suggests that the company is vaguely sorry the customer might have been put to some trouble, but admits no fault and promises nothing. Such phrases are not apologies, and they do nothing to reduce customer anger and disappointment.

Why, then, do companies use such insincere catchphrases? Typically, it's because they don't want to be openly rude but don't want to admit fault, either. In particular, huge corporations use these phrases because they make their money on volume and can easily afford to lose individual customers. Canned catchphrases give a company's customer service representatives something to say when faced with an irate customer but make no commitments on the company's behalf. The subtext of these phrases usually amounts to this: "We're big enough that we don't really need your money, and we're not going to change our business practices just because you don't like what we do." That may be true, but it's rarely what your customers want to hear.

Be specific. Unhappy consumers want to know they've been heard, so be sure to address your customers' concerns as specifically as you possibly can. Here's a great example of an extremely effective apology delivered by the Walt Disney Corporation, a company with an outstanding reputation for customer service:

Margot was excited to make her first trip to Disney World with her family but was deeply disappointed to discover that the automated "hostess" of one of the shows at the park was a blonde, Barbie-like mannequin in fishnet stockings and fluttering lashes. Margot thought the character was likely to confuse little girls and perpetuate sexist stereotypes. She wrote a letter to Disney expressing her concerns. A few weeks later, Margot was surprised and delighted to receive a personalized letter from Disney's vice president for "Imagineering" that addressed every one of her points in detail and assured her of the company's commitment to providing its customers with the highest quality of family entertainment. Margot felt that Disney had taken her concerns seriously and responded thoughtfully, and came away deeply impressed with the company and a bigger fan than ever. (Incidentally, the character she objected to has long since disappeared, suggesting that Disney really listened to customer feedback and adapted its product to their tastes.)

It's also a good idea to be very clear and specific about what you'll do to prevent mistakes from happening again. In one famous incident, JetBlue was forced to apologize to customers on planes that had been held up to eleven hours on the tarmac at JFK Airport in New York when a snowstorm enveloped the region. Ultimately, the company's CEO was replaced, and JetBlue issued a "customer bill of rights" to deal with similar future incidents. While the incident may have temporarily damaged JetBlue's previously excellent reputation, its very specific promise to do better was certainly an essential element of an effective corporate apology.

Make extra amends. While the occasional irate customer or client makes excessive demands, most people consider a reasonable attempt to make things right to be sufficient. If, for example, a restaurant overcooks a steak, the average diner expects no more than to get another steak, properly cooked, sometime before his dining companions finish their entrees. You certainly could stop there, but your customer would still have been put to the inconvenience of waiting for his food while others ate, or the embarrassment of watching his companions' food cool, uneaten, until his new steak arrived. So, why not give a little more and offer free desserts or a round of beverages to compensate for the inconvenience? Even if your customer declines the extra benefit, he'll appreciate your thoughtfulness and probably come back for another meal.

Professional Malpractice

Professionals such as doctors, lawyers, clergy, engineers, and accountants occupy a special position of trust and respect that society recognizes in its laws (allowing only licensed practitioners to provide many professional services) and, often, better-than-average compensation. Their clients—or patients, in the case of medical professionals—trust them with their lives, their health, their finances, and their property. Clients expect their professional advisors to be honest and competent, to devote enough time to their affairs to bring them to a satisfactory conclusion, and to exercise good professional judgment. When mistakes are made, clients of these professionals may feel and express a sense of personal betrayal that a merchant's customer never would.

Professionals typically are also more invested in their clients' well-being than a shopkeeper might be. They're normally bound by professional codes of ethics, and recognize that they have a special obligation to apply their special expertise—often acquired through years of rigorous professional education and experience—with integrity, skill, and care. Yes, some would-be professionals enroll in graduate school in the expectation of receiving a well-paid job with their diploma, but many more enter their chosen profession in the hope of making the world a better place.

Unfortunately, great skills are all too often accompanied by great egos, and some professionals have a very hard time admitting to error, much less apologizing for it. When professionals do make mistakes, they may be at higher risk of being sued by their clients than a non-professional would be (more about that below), and that can provide an additional disincentive for a professional to apologize. However, most professionals value their own integrity and their clients' interests highly enough that they won't withhold an apology if one is due. If you're a professional in the position of owing an apology to a client, here are some things to keep in mind:

Speak simply. Most professionals are trained to use highly specialized language that can be difficult for a client to understand. Lawyers and doctors use Latin, accountants and actuaries use mathematical terms of art, and engineers and scientists may use technical terms no layperson can possibly comprehend. When apologizing to a client, don't hide behind incomprehensible jargon, which to your client may sound like evasive gobbledygook. Explain what happened in plain language, and use analogies, photographs, or even drawings to get your point across. Suppose, for example, that you're a cardiologist who has to explain to a patient's family why a complicated operation went awry. Using a model of the heart or likening it to a water pump might be useful in helping the family understand what went wrong.

Focus on the client. For some professionals, a mistake is so personally embarrassing that they forget who has been injured. In one case in which a renowned surgeon was working quickly, he made a careless mistake, and the patient died on the operating table. The surgeon's "apology" to the family consisted of a several-minute rant of disbelief that he could have done something so amateurish, during which he failed even to note their shock and pain. Needless to say, the apology was far from effective.

Be respectful. If you're not accustomed to making significant mistakes, you may be uncomfortable with having to admit your human fallibility. Suppose you're an attorney who just lost a client's case because you hadn't prepared properly for the trial, and you're feeling extremely defensive about it. Resist the temptation to get up on your high horse to deflect blame or to be dismissive and act as if the client's loss was no big deal. If your client deserves an apology from you, she also deserves to hear it delivered with appropriate humility.

Take steps to prevent future errors. When professionals make mistakes, the consequences in terms of money, health, and even life can be particularly severe. As a result, when clients get hurt by a professional, they're often especially interested in hearing what the professional will do to prevent anyone else from suffering a similar injury. Imagine, for example, that a pediatrician underestimated the seriousness of a baby's fever, failing to hospitalize the child until he was seriously dehydrated and had suffered permanent brain injury. Although nothing could restore their child to perfect health, the baby's parents would undoubtedly be particularly glad to hear that the doctor had established a new protocol requiring any infant who ran a fever for more than forty-eight hours to be treated for dehydration as a precautionary measure.

Can Apologies Prevent Lawsuits?

No discussion of business apologies would be complete without an acknowledgment that, at least in the United States, mistakes in business all too frequently end up being addressed in court. When wrongs are committed in personal relationships, lawsuits are unlikely, in part because both parties are emotionally involved and usually hope to maintain the relationship. (Suits for divorce are an exception.) In business, by contrast, there's generally less personal loyalty involved and, even worse, often a real financial incentive to use a company's mistake as an opportunity for financial gain. Lawsuits drive up the price of the food we eat, the fuel we buy, the dry goods we purchase, and the services we use. Indeed, some experts estimate that the average family of four pays over $2,000 per year in hidden costs associated with business litigation.

People who have been injured by someone else's carelessness or deliberate misconduct should, of course, be compensated. Their anger and hurt are usually justified and need to be recognized and respected, and if the injury has altered their life's course, financial compensation is often the only possible way to make amends for their losses. At the same time, does it really serve anyone's best interests to turn people's private tragedies into public sideshows? And is litigation necessarily the best way to ensure that injured people get the compensation they deserve?

Having worked as an attorney for more than twenty years, I have tremendous respect for the American judicial system. However, I have also seen the terrible toll litigation takes on everyone involved. Our legal system is what lawyers call "adversarial," which means that it presumes that the parties involved in a legal dispute are irreconcilable enemies, who can resolve their differences only by having their attorneys fight it out in court. Like knights in armor slashing each other with swords and axes, the lawyers battle to win for their clients, often at a staggering cost in time, effort, and money.

How litigation works. As a first step in explaining how apologies can affect lawsuits, a grossly oversimplified description of how litigation works follows. (Please do *not* take this as individual legal advice, because it isn't. If you or your company is facing a lawsuit, talk to a lawyer about your situation before taking action.)

When an individual suffers an injury, the American legal system offers that individual (usually called the "plaintiff") a venue in which to seek restitution for an injury from the person or entity (usually called the "defendant") that the plaintiff thinks caused the injury. The courts don't just take liability for granted, though; in most instances, before a plaintiff can collect restitution from the defendant, the plaintiff's attorney has to prove several things:

- that the defendant owed the plaintiff a legally enforceable duty—this usually amounts to a duty not to be careless, dishonest, or malicious, or to provide expected goods or services as promised;

- that the defendant breached that duty by acting carelessly, dishonestly, maliciously, or not as promised;

- that the defendant's actions injured the plaintiff;

- that the plaintiff is therefore entitled to compensation; and

- how much compensation it will take to make the plaintiff whole.

Typically, the defendant doesn't have to prove a thing until the plaintiff has persuaded a court that he has a valid case. However, most defense attorneys don't sit idly by waiting for the plaintiff's counsel to come up short in front of the judge. Defense lawyers go into every case thinking carefully about their strategy, and usually it includes refusing to say or do anything to make the job of the plaintiff's attorney any easier, particularly if it involves admitting to error.

There are several ways to prove in court that a defendant breached a duty to the plaintiff, but one of the easiest ways is to show that the defendant actually admitted to having done something wrong. That is why defense lawyers usually tell their clients not to apologize to disappointed customers or clients who sue them.

Apologies and litigation. One of the six essential elements of an effective apology is taking responsibility for your mistakes. From your defense attorney's perspective, however, taking responsibility is essentially the same as admitting that you breached your duty of care. Your doing so makes the plaintiff's case that much easier to prove, and makes it that much harder for the defense attorney to win.

Many lawyers, therefore, consider it tantamount to malpractice to advise their clients to apologize to a disappointed client or customer. From a purely defensive, legal perspective, they usually have an excellent point. After all, if you don't take responsibility for a mistake that you've made, the plaintiff can't use your own words against you in a lawsuit.

From a larger, more human perspective, however, legalistic silence may not be your best approach. Once you and your company have gotten into a defensive legal posture, it becomes very difficult to stop the adversarial process. However, a well-timed and effective apology that takes into account all six of the essential elements can fend off the blame-and-shame cycle, and can even prevent lawsuits from being filed in the first place. Here's an example of one case in which a professional's apology protected him from a potentially expensive and embarrassing lawsuit:

Eric was a professional advisor to a pension plan that covered the employees of a small town. During contract negotiations with the employees' union, the town government, which sponsored the plan, asked Eric to estimate the potential costs to the town of providing dozens of different kinds of employment and retirement benefits. Everyone understood that Eric would be providing only rough estimates and that he would be working to meet tight deadlines. Eric made a good effort but, in the process of completing so many complicated calculations so quickly, he significantly underestimated the cost of one of the many benefits that the town and the union ultimately agreed to include in their collective bargaining agreement.

Eric realized what he had done a few weeks after the labor negotiations were completed, and the agreement between the union and
the town had been signed. He recognized that admitting to his mistake could increase his risk of being sued, but he decided that he
could not in good conscience allow his mistake to go unreported. He
also realized that his mistake would probably be discovered at some
point anyway, so he was facing a potential lawsuit whether he admitted to his mistake or not. After determining the correct cost of the
benefit, Eric contacted the government officials who had hired him,
explained what had happened, and apologized for the error. The town
officials were understandably unhappy to discover that they had
agreed to a benefit that would cost the town more than they had
anticipated, and there was some talk of bringing a malpractice suit
against Eric. Ultimately, however, Eric's straightforward apology
stood him in good stead. By coming forward so quickly, he made it
easier for the town government and the union to mitigate the effects
of his mistake, and everyone involved was impressed by Eric's
integrity. The town officials decided that the town could afford to
offer the benefit, and chose not to sue Eric, privately praising him for
his honesty and courage.

Eric's story demonstrates that one of the benefits of an effective
apology can be to persuade a disappointed client or customer not to
sue you. This is not, of course, the primary reason to apologize. As in
any other situation, the primary purpose of an apology is to make
things right with the disappointed customer or client—the focus
should be on that person's interests, not on yours. If you make a good-
faith effort to figure out how to make things right, however, you may
find, as Eric did, that the other party comes away with such a high
opinion of you that he or she wouldn't dream of giving you a hard
time in court.

The medical profession in particular has made great strides
toward using apologies effectively and, thereby, reducing litigation

risk. Doctors typically feel a tremendous responsibility toward their patients, and often chafe under legal advice to remain silent after a patient suffers a medical injury. Consequently, more hospitals and physicians are moving away from stiff-arming patients and families when a medical error occurs, instead opting to apologize for the error, offer amends, and explain the specific procedural steps that will be taken to prevent other patients from suffering similarly. That approach has strengthened the doctor-patient bond, reduced hospitals' overall litigation costs, and freed their attorneys to vigorously defend truly frivolous malpractice lawsuits. Recognizing the social benefits of this approach, several states have passed "apology" laws that make it easier for medical practitioners to apologize in the wake of an error.

Unfortunately, corporate America has yet to catch up with the medical and other professions when it comes to reducing litigation risk by making apologies. That may be true in part because big corporations have so many customers that their lawyers are afraid to apologize to individual patrons for fear of inviting a deluge of copycat lawsuits if the apology becomes public. One of the most famous recent examples of a company refusing to even discuss reasonable restitution occurred when an elderly woman suffered third-degree burns after spilling a cup of McDonald's coffee into her lap. Her family attempted repeatedly to settle the case, asking for $20,000 to cover her $11,000 of medical bills and to provide some small compensation for her pain and suffering. The McDonald's legal team refused, offering less than $1,000 to compensate the injured woman.

McDonald's paid dearly for its tactics. Faced with significant medical bills, the woman's family took the fast-food giant to court. Testimony at the trial revealed that the company had excellent reason to know that its coffee was served extremely, perhaps even dangerously, hot, and had refused to allow local restaurants to serve it cooler even after receiving numerous complaints. The case made headlines when the jury awarded the injured woman $200,000 to compensate her for her injuries, and then walloped McDonald's with a $2.7 million punitive damage assessment (an amount that the jury reckoned to be roughly equal to two days' revenue from McDonald's coffee sales). The judge ultimately reduced the total damages awarded to the injured woman to approximately $640,000, but McDonald's still suffered not only a financial loss but also a tremendous hit to its reputation with the public. The case became a flashpoint for litigation reform discussions in the United States and remains a blot on the company's name.

Should You Apologize When a Lawsuit Is Imminent?

Every situation is different, but if a client or customer is threatening to sue you, making an effective apology might save you a lot of time, money, and personal pain. If you think apologizing is the way to go, there are some things you should keep in mind.

Get your lawyer involved right away. Apologizing before you've thought through what you're going to say can cause you tremendous trouble later in court. Fortunately, a good lawyer can often help you develop an apology that will mend fences without unreasonably compromising your legal position. If you find yourself in a situation in which you or your company is facing a potential dispute with a client or customer and there is a significant amount of money at stake, it's a good idea to talk to your lawyer up front. If a disappointed customer or client is threatening to sue you, make sure to consult your attorney before you apologize in person or, particularly, in writing. As Eric's case demonstrated and as the medical profession is finding, an effective apology can go a long way toward preventing a lawsuit, but when litigation is in the offing, an apology needs to be carefully considered. For very good reasons, your lawyer's first instinct will probably be to tell you not to apologize at all, so that you don't accidentally admit to liability. Don't get impatient—your lawyer is simply warning you of potential litigation risks, which is exactly what you pay him or her to do. However, if your own instincts tell you that an apology to a client or customer is the right way to go, work with your lawyer to develop an apology that will do the job without significantly increasing your litigation risk.

Check the terms of your insurance. While many businesses and professions are starting to appreciate that effective apologies can stave off litigation, insurance companies haven't all gotten the message. If you, or your company, carry professional or business liability coverage, the terms of your policy may limit your ability to apologize when faced with the possibility of litigation. (You may even discover that your insurance company has reserved the exclusive right to defend you.) It may be that you'll decide to apologize anyway, but it's a good idea to know going in whether making an apology will void your coverage or not.

Apologize before the lawsuit is filed. Unfortunately, businesses and professionals frequently take too long to recognize that they're facing a potentially serious lawsuit. Consequently, they apologize late, if at all, adding fuel to the angry customer's ire. Yes, you can still apologize after the papers have been filed, but by then you'll already have started to incur legal fees, and at least some harm will already be done to your business's reputation. Once you've decided to apologize, don't wait for the grass to grow—or for the court documents to land on your desk.

Be creative about making amends. While this advice almost always applies when you're making an apology, it can be particularly important when you're facing potential litigation. Why? Because money alone isn't always enough to repair a business or professional error, but lawyers may tend to default to money damages as the obvious remedy. If you get creative, however, it's more likely that your lawyer will, too. In one great example, a hospital worked with a patient who had been partially disabled by a medical error to find an appropriate way to make amends. The patient's family, after much soul-searching, decided that the patient really needed a mobile home, and the hospital agreed to provide it. The mobile home didn't come cheap, but it was much less expensive than a lawsuit would have been, and the patient got what he truly needed to live well.

Don't delay needed repairs. Sometimes companies are reluctant to make necessary changes when a mistake occurs because they're afraid their corrective actions will be used against them in court. To use a classic law school example, imagine that a customer slips and falls on the front stairs of your shop, injuring herself severely. You discover that one of the steps is loose, which is probably why she fell. You might be afraid to fix the steps because you think the fact that you repaired them would help your customer prove the steps were dangerous to begin with. Fortunately, the legal system recognizes the benefits of rectifying unsafe situations, so most courts won't accept evidence of subsequent repairs. It's probably a good idea to touch base with your lawyer first, but if you have unsafe conditions on your premises, it's usually better to correct them than to risk additional injury to anyone else.

Make corrective measures a permanent part of the culture. As with all apologies, it's important to make sure you continue to do better after an apology. Too often, however, companies put corrective measures into place, but fail to cement them with proper staff training and follow-up. Let's say, for example, that your financial firm was responsible for putting together a complex investment analysis report for an important client. The analyst who put the report together worked too quickly to meet the deadline and neglected to have a peer within your company check the report over before sending it to your client. As a result, the analysis contained several key errors, but the client relied on it to invest—and lose—a lot of money. Telling that analyst to slow down and get peer review in the future is a good idea, but it's not likely to make a major change in your company's culture. Putting a formal peer review policy in place and regularly training all of your employees on what's expected is much more likely to prevent similar mistakes in the future.

When You Want to Apologize, but Your Company Doesn't

Even if you've come to believe in the power of apologies to prevent litigation, you may not always be able to put that belief into action. There are several reasons a large company might not want to issue an apology:

- The amount of money involved makes the risks seem too great;

- corporate counsel is dead set against it;

- apologies aren't part of the corporate culture;

- senior management thinks the threat of litigation will blow over faster without an apology.

If you're in a situation in which you think your company owes an apology to a client or customer, but others disagree, there are still things you can do. Imagine, for instance, that you're the manager of a local branch of a national restaurant chain. One evening, several customers become extremely ill after eating in your restaurant, seven are hospitalized, and two die. The outbreak could have been caused by tainted vegetables from your local supplier, but there was also some uncertainty about whether you had been cooking meat to the recommended temperature. You've been following the national corporation's rules on cooking techniques, so there may be a larger question of whether consumers nationwide have been put at risk by the corporation's practices. The national corporate office ordered you and your employees to refuse all comment on the matter, and the company's legal team warned you that any statement on your part, and particularly an apology to any of the victims or their families, could be taken as an admission of responsibility that could cost the company millions of dollars and put your individual restaurant out of business.

In such a situation, you'd probably be unable to apologize, at least right away. You still have several options, however.

Press for a corporate apology. If you're in a position to do so, encourage the corporate office and its attorneys to issue an apology, and help make it an effective one. It may not feel as good to you as a personal apology would, but it will do more to mend fences with the victims and their families than a blanket denial of responsibility from your company would.

Cooperate. Be as forthcoming as possible with the people in your company who are assigned to investigate the incident. (This isn't the same as talking to the press—when it comes to media matters, defer to the advice of your company's media experts.) Don't try to cover up what happened and, to the extent you can, discourage any attempt on the part of corporate management to do so. The truth will come out eventually, and you and your company will look far better if you do all you can to make it happen.

Apologize at last. Once the matter has been resolved (and that could take years, especially if the matter ends up in court), you may want to follow up with a personal apology to the people who were injured. It probably won't be as effective as it would have been had you been able to apologize right away, but even a belated apology may be appreciated by the injured parties, and it may help you feel better about the incident as well.

*   *   *   *

Sometimes companies find themselves in situations in which they have to apologize not just to individual plaintiffs, but to a huge segment of their customer base or even the public as a whole. If you find yourself in such a situation, and you or your company has to make a public apology, take a look at Chapter 10 ("Public Apologies") for some ideas on how to make your apology as effective as possible.

CHAPTER 8

Apologizing to Loved Ones

There's one sad truth in life I've found
While journeying east and west—
The only folks we really wound
Are those we love the best.

—ELLA WHEELER WILCOX

As difficult as it can be to apologize in a business setting, apologies to loved ones can be even more challenging for several reasons. Emotions are usually far more intense in personal relationships than in business, which means injuries are more painful and difficult to remedy. Other people tend to get involved—family members, friends, and business associates—and can be particularly unforgiving of slights inflicted on their loved ones. A person with a reputation for being a ruthless business competitor may be tolerated or even grudgingly admired professionally, but if that same person swindles a friend, cheats on his or her spouse, lies to a parent, or abuses a child, no one is likely to applaud the traits that make him good at his job. These and other considerations can make it especially difficult to apologize to someone you hold dear. So, before you plunge into such an apology, carefully review the advice in this chapter.

The Special Challenges of Apologizing to Your Loved Ones

Loved ones know you well—perhaps too well. They usually have a keen awareness of the full range of your shortcomings based on years of close observation. The longer they've known you, the more aware they are of your past mistakes and persistent faults. It can be very difficult to persuade someone who's known you well for a long time that you're ever going to change long-standing patterns of behavior. When you apologize for a fresh mistake, it's usually not surprising when your loved one reminds you of a similar mistake you made days, months, or even years before. It's entirely too easy to get defensive when you know that an apology might provoke a recitation of every peccadillo you've ever committed.

Most important, though, a personal relationship with a parent, spouse, child, or even a good friend is normally expected to last a lifetime. Losing a friend, having a parent or child cut off contact with you, or divorcing a spouse is not only painful in the short term, it can be emotionally devastating for years, if not for the rest of your life. In business, by contrast, it's commonplace for people to change jobs, consultants, and clients several times in a career, so a mistake among colleagues usually won't haunt you forever.

Let's say, for example, that you got to gossiping with a co-worker and, in a weak moment, made a nasty comment about the college student who was hired as the company's summer intern, calling her "cute enough, but dumb as a box of rocks." If overheard or repeated, that comment would certainly hurt the intern's feelings and might get you in hot water with human resources, but the incident probably wouldn't have a lasting impact on your life once the summer ended and the intern went back to college. If you made the same snide wisecrack to your spouse about your daughter, however, and your daughter overheard it, she would probably be devastated. It might take years before she matured enough to believe that you really didn't mean what you said, and your relationship might never fully recover.

Recognizing, then, that the stakes are often particularly high when you apologize to a loved one, how can you maximize the chances that your apology will be effective? Here are some strategies to keep in mind.

Don't take forgiveness for granted. When you're dealing with a loved one, it's easy to make the mistake of thinking that the other person will be particularly forgiving because of your established relationship. That would be nice, but it often isn't true. If anything, loved ones may be even less forgiving than casual acquaintances because they have so much more at stake in the relationship and so much more potential for pain. Review the six essential elements of an effective apology in Chapter 3, and make sure they're all included in any apology you make to a loved one. In particular, be sure to express appreciation for your loved one's presence in your life. If, for example, you're apologizing to an old friend for missing her wedding, be sure to tell her how grateful you are to have had her as a friend for so many years, and how much you wish you could be there to share in her special day. Your apology will be much more effective if your loved one knows you don't take his or her love and support for granted.

Don't get caught in a blame loop. The fact that you love someone doesn't mean you find that person easy to live with, and the same old arguments have an ugly way of coming up again and again. Let's say, for example, that your husband left his wet towel on the bed for what seemed to you to be the hundredth time this week, and you exploded at him. When you apologize for shouting, don't try to shift the blame to him by pointing out that you wouldn't have shouted if he'd just put his wet towel in the laundry instead of leaving it on the bed again. You've already had that discussion many times, and if he thinks you're only apologizing to get him to change, your apology will fail. Just apologize for your own behavior, and wait until you've both had a chance to cool down to talk to him about why you object to wet towels on your bed.

Don't insist on an immediate return apology. Apologies delivered on demand are rarely effective, and that's especially true between loved ones. Let's say, for example, that your wife's father started talking politics at a family dinner and said several things that you found offensive. When you politely disagreed with him, your wife took his side, leaving you feeling angry and unsupported, so you lost your temper and abruptly left the table. Driving home in strained silence, you decide to apologize for your outburst. But you might as well not even bother if your apology to your wife amounts to, "I'm sorry I lost my temper, but now you need to apologize to me for taking sides against me with your father. And oh, by the way, I don't know why you even married me, since you still seem to be Daddy's little girl." She'll probably refuse to apologize as a matter of principle, and you'll be well on your way to another, uglier fight. Just apologize for your own behavior. If you apologize effectively, your wife may apologize to you on her own, and you'll be able to talk together about how to handle her father with more aplomb. If she doesn't reciprocate, and you want to ask your wife for an apology, read "How to Ask for an Apology" (Chapter 11) first.

Give it extra time. It's always a good idea to give someone whom you've hurt or offended some time to forgive you, but it's particularly important in a close relationship. Remember, your loved one cares about you enough to really suffer if you hurt or offend him or her, so it will probably take your loved one longer to get over an offense than it would take someone else. Let's say, for example, that when your best friend asked if she looked fat in a new dress, you jokingly said, yes, it made her look like a baby whale. Your comment might not bother someone else very much, but if your friend valued your opinion enough to ask you, she was probably really hurt by what you said. After you've apologized, take it easy with her for a while longer than you might with someone else.

Go the extra mile to make amends. When you have to make amends with a loved one, you'll probably need to do more to fully restore his or her trust than you would in a more casual relationship. This isn't a matter of spending money—if anything, spending money in a personal relationship may be even riskier than it is in a more casual one. Let's say, for example, that you forgot your wife's birthday for the third year in a row. Buying an extra dozen roses isn't likely to enhance the probability that your sheepish apology will earn you forgiveness. In fact, your wife may be even angrier that you thought you could buy her off. Instead, be thoughtful—what would be a really meaningful way to show your love and your desire to make things right? Your wife might welcome an afternoon to herself while you watch the kids, the freedom to spend a full Saturday with her best friend while you handle the housework, a home-cooked meal that you prepared, or an evening of your undivided attention far more than any expensive gift you could buy.

Mind your manners. Because the emotional stakes are so often elevated when you apologize to a loved one, it's especially important to keep your own negative emotions in check. As you apologize, make sure you're entirely sincere and genuinely repentant. This is not the time for jokes, defensiveness, double-talk, or self-pity. When you do whatever you decide is appropriate to make amends, don't pout, don't argue, and don't try to get out of it. Remember, the loved one you've hurt is someone who really matters to you, so be glad to have the opportunity to make things right. Even if you think what you did wasn't all that bad, your apology won't be effective unless your words, manner, and action clearly prove that you're trying to make things right. Let's suppose, for example, that you've never especially liked your brother's girlfriend, and you gave into temptation and got into an argument with her at a family party. You and your brother have agreed that the best way for you to make amends with him is to take his girlfriend to lunch and apologize to her in person. Invite her politely, take her to a nice place, and follow the advice in Chapter 3 ("The Six Essential Elements of an Effective Apology") when you apologize to her. Then be pleasant for the rest of the meal—no sarcasm, eye rolling, or other put-downs. Remember, your brother loves this woman enough to want you to mend fences with her even more than he wants you to apologize to him. That means it's important for you to respect his feelings for her and put your own aside. If you let your dislike for her get the better of you again, your apology will fail, and you'll do lasting harm not only to your relationship with the girlfriend but also to your brother's trust in you.

Don't delay. A wise, anonymous author once wrote, "Present your family and friends with their eulogies now—they won't be able to hear how much you love and appreciate them from inside the coffin." The same holds true for apologies. The longer you wait to apologize to a loved one, the harder apologizing will become and the more damage you're likely to do. Let's say, for example, that your grandfather lives in a nursing home and you haven't visited him for over a year. Don't compound your neglect by failing to apologize while he's still healthy enough to hear and forgive you. Make the time, go visit, and tell him you're sorry you didn't get there sooner.

If you offended in public, apologize publicly. While this is always a good rule to follow, it can be tempting to break it when you're apologizing to a loved one, but it's not smart to give in to that temptation. Just as you shouldn't take forgiveness for granted in a personal relationship, you shouldn't assume that a loved one will necessarily get over a public embarrassment any faster just because he or she loves you. Let's say, for example, that your wife and children threw a massive surprise party for your fortieth birthday. You posted pictures from the party on your Facebook page that clearly showed how much you enjoyed the bash but accompanied them with a post saying, "I wanted golf clubs for my birthday, and all I got was this stupid party!" Although you just meant to be funny, your family saw the post as a rejection of all the time and effort they put into the celebration, and their feelings were clearly hurt. Apologize to them in person, but don't stop there. Put up another post saying something like, "Age has clearly addled my brain! Apologies and thanks to my wonderful wife and kids for a celebration I'll never forget. It was a fantastic surprise, and I love you!" In doing so, you'll cover your bases in private and public, too.

Apologizing When Age Is a Factor

Apologizing to a loved one who is a peer, whether a sibling, a close friend, or your partner, can be difficult enough, but when age becomes a factor, the situation can be even harder. You may find yourself in a position in which you have to apologize to a loved one who's much younger or older than you are. Here are some things to keep in mind.

Apologizing to children. It's a cliché, but kids are people too, and they usually have very well developed ideas about what is and isn't fair. It can be tempting to brush off a child's anger or hurt feelings with the theory that the child will "get over it." However, failing to treat a child with the same respect that you would show to an adult can do lasting damage to your relationship and to the child's self-esteem. If you have to apologize to a child, don't kid yourself into thinking that you can get off lightly. If you truly want to restore that child's trust, you'll need to include all six of the essential elements in your apology, and take into account a few potential pitfalls.

Don't talk down. Children don't like being condescended to any more than adults do. If you're apologizing to a child, don't try the "because I'm a grown-up and I know better" routine. If you really knew better, you wouldn't need to apologize. Admit to your mistake as directly as you would when talking to an adult, and make sure your apology is sincere and straightforward.

Get eye to eye. Sit, squat, or put the child on a step stool—find a way to get on the same physical level as the child when you apologize. This is another way to avoid talking down. It demonstrates your respect for the child and your willingness to admit your mistakes, both of which are key to an effective apology.

Get to the point. Kids tend to have shorter attention spans than adults do, so don't prolong your apology. Use simple language and say everything you need to without hesitating or talking in circles. Not only will your apology be more effective, you'll be teaching the child that it's all right to make mistakes if you admit to what you've done and apologize. Ultimately, that may be one of the best lessons you can teach.

Apologizing to the elderly. Sometimes you have to apologize to a parent, grandparent, or other person who's significantly older than you are. These apologies can be particularly tricky for several reasons. Too often, seniors in our society get treated like children, which can make them feel disrespected and justifiably resentful. Additionally, seniors sometimes have health issues that make it difficult to talk to them or difficult for them to remember what you've said. If you have to apologize to a senior, take the same care that you would with anyone else to include all six essential elements of an apology, and keep a few additional points in mind.

Speak up. Seniors frequently complain that young people aren't as well spoken as they used to be, and they have a point. (If you doubt that, rent a few old movies and listen to how clearly actors used to speak.) Don't shout or slow down too much—you don't want to create the impression that you think the other person is deaf or dim-witted—but pay a little extra attention to your enunciation.

Be patient. Even if you're a middle-aged adult with a successful professional career, you probably seem like a kid to the older person. You've already done something that hurt or offended him, and probably injured his dignity in the process. Don't compound your mistake by cutting the conversation short if he starts commenting on your past mistakes or telling you at length exactly what you did wrong. Just bite your tongue and recognize that part of making amends is listening to whatever the other person has to say.

Repeat as necessary. If the older person has become forgetful, he or she may not even remember your apology, or may remember it very differently after a while than you do. Again, be patient, and clarify what you said or apologize again if you need to do so. Remember, your goal is to mend your relationship with this person, so do what you must to make matters right.

* * * *

The intensity of relationships with friends and family can make apologizing especially difficult, but that's also why these apologies are so important. Ultimately, your most cherished memories are likely to be of the time you spent with the people you loved best. An effective apology to a loved one can work wonders to keep your relationship with that person strong.

CHAPTER 9

Apologizing to Casual Contacts

Never lose sight of the fact that the most important yardstick of your success will be how you treat other people—your family, friends, and co-workers, and even strangers you meet along the way.

—BARBARA BUSH

As we go through our complex, stressful daily lives, it's inevitable that we step on strangers' toes now and then. Whether you're fighting your way to work during rush hour, hurrying to get an errand done at the drugstore, or waiting in seemingly endless lines at the Department of Motor Vehicles, it's easy to get stressed out and to become impatient. When that happens, accidental insults to strangers, or even downright rudeness, are likely to follow, and you may not be certain how to apologize.

For example, let's say you're running late to work one morning and cut someone off in traffic. If the other person is late and stressed as well, you may become the victim of a road rage incident if you don't find a way to make things right. You can't exactly get out of your car in the middle of the road to apologize, however, so you have to come up with another way to handle the situation.

Apologies to casual acquaintances fall in a similar category. When you know someone only slightly, you don't know how the other person will react to an offense. An apology that seems perfectly adequate to you may fall far short with someone who takes your initial mistake more seriously than you would. Suppose, for example, that at a party you foolishly decided to tell a politically incorrect joke to someone whom you didn't know very well, and the other person was offended by it. If you don't find an appropriate way to apologize, you may lose a potential friend. If the other person is sufficiently offended, your host may even get an earful about your boorish behavior the next day, which could do lasting damage to your friendship with him as well.

Awkward situations come up every day when groups of people, strangers and acquaintances alike, are out in the world living their daily lives. This chapter covers what to do when your path collides in an unfortunate way with someone else's.

The Basics of Apologizing to Strangers and Casual Acquaintances

It may not seem immediately obvious, but you can apologize effectively to someone you don't know, or don't know very well, when the need arises. Doing so usually requires you to touch certain key bases.

Act fast. When you're dealing with a stranger or casual acquaintance, the window of opportunity to apologize is brief. Let's use the bad joke at the party as an example: If you don't apologize as soon as you realize you've offended the other person, you're not likely to get a second chance. That person's bad opinion of you could harden in seconds, and he or she may walk away from you, in which case your opportunity is probably lost. Say you're sorry right away—don't let the moment pass.

Don't get fancy. You won't have time to polish your apology, so keep it as simple and straightforward as possible. Otherwise, you run the risk of being misunderstood or having the other person think you're being sarcastic. Keep it to a few plain words, such as, "I shouldn't have made that joke—I'm so sorry." Anything more is likely to be too much. If the other person is receptive to your apology, you'll have an additional opportunity to explain if necessary. If he or she is not, at least you'll have made the attempt to make things right.

Keep your cool. The other person really doesn't know anything about you except that you've just done something hurtful or offensive, so he or she probably won't be inclined to cut you a lot of slack. Consequently, he or she may react more strongly than you think is appropriate. In such cases, even if you think you're right, don't make things worse by getting testy in return. If you stay calm and are sincerely apologetic, the other person will probably calm down pretty quickly, too. For example, let's say you spill a drink on the man next to you in a movie theater. Apologize immediately, offer him a handkerchief or napkin to mop up the mess (don't try to help him clean up—if you're a stranger, your touch probably won't be welcome), and don't say a word if he calls you a nasty name or says something rude in return.

Don't defend yourself. If you hurt or anger someone you don't know well, you'll probably want to persuade the other person that you're really not so bad by explaining why you acted the way you did. Don't do it. As we'll see in Chapter 15 ("The Thirteen Most Common Ways to Botch an Apology"), nothing ruins a good apology faster than making excuses. You don't have enough goodwill built up with the other person to expect him or her to stand there and listen patiently while you rationalize, so don't even try.

Back off. If your offense is that you've taken something that the other person was entitled to, give it back immediately. Let's say, for example, that you pulled into an open space in a crowded parking lot before realizing that another driver had been waiting for it. Pull out, let the other driver take the space, wait for him to get out of his car, and then make your apology. You may have to wait a little longer to get to your business, but you'll have done the right thing, and maybe averted a nasty encounter with the other driver in the process.

The same principle applies in traffic. Let's return to the example from the beginning of this chapter: If you accidentally cut someone off while driving, try to get out of the other driver's way as soon as you can (don't compound your mistake by cutting off someone else, though). You won't be in a position to tell the other person you're sorry, but you can show your remorse by yielding the lane.

Go the extra mile. If the circumstances seem right, consider whether you can do a little something more for the other person to strengthen your apology. Let's say, for example, that you cut ahead of an elderly woman in the supermarket checkout line. After you've apologized and given her back her place in line, offer to help her take her groceries to her car. If she turns down your offer of help, that's fine—at least you made the attempt. If she accepts and lets you help her, you'll know you've made things right with her, and you can both go about the rest of your day in a better mood.

Even if you can't do something extra right away, you may have an opportunity to do the other person a favor sometime in the future. For example, suppose your hairstylist cut your hair shorter than you like, and you got unreasonably angry about it. Once you calmed down, and your hair grew out a little, you realized that you needed to apologize for your overreaction. After making the apology, you might want to look for opportunities to help your hairstylist out, perhaps by complimenting him to his manager or referring a few friends to him. Making that extra effort will demonstrate that you're genuinely sorry, and will probably strengthen your relationship.

Don't expect thanks. Even if you think you've apologized adequately and that your mistake wasn't all that bad to begin with, don't be surprised or offended if the other person responds badly to your attempt to apologize. Return to the example of the elderly lady in the grocery store: You might think that cutting ahead of her in line was just an innocent oversight, but she, on the other hand, may see your mistake as proof that no one respects or appreciates her now that she's gotten older, and may continue to be angry with you even after you've done everything you can to apologize. If that happens, it will be because the other person has concerns you know nothing about and can't address. Let it go, and get on with your day.

Reap the Benefits

Why should you even care if you've offended a stranger? For one thing, you never know when you might run into that person again. That stranger might be a potential friend, employer, client, or even sweetheart that you could lose tomorrow if you don't apologize today. Another reason is that the other person might retaliate against you. In a memorable scene in the movie *Fried Green Tomatoes*, a pair of teenage girls cut in front of Kathy Bates's character to claim a parking space, then made a snide remark about being "younger and faster" as they walked away. The Bates character responded by slamming her car repeatedly into theirs, wrapping up with, "Face it, girls, I'm older and I have more insurance." An on-the-spot apology might have kept the girls' fender intact.

You may also want to apologize as a matter of personal integrity. If you owe someone an apology, you should deliver it even if the other person isn't someone you're likely to see again. If you don't apologize, you'll carry with you the discomfort of having fallen short. On the other hand, if you apologize and make amends, you can put your slipup behind you and be comfortable that you've behaved well.

Perhaps the best reason to apologize to strangers and casual acquaintances, though, is that you'll contribute a little civility to the world. We have a choice, individually and collectively, of whether we're going to treat one another kindly or not. Apologizing when you make a mistake is a basic courtesy, and a small price to pay to help make the society we share more pleasant.

*   *   *   *

If you have to apologize to friends, family, or business associates, it will probably be because you've made a fairly significant mistake that needs a thoughtful, well-timed apology. By contrast, most of the mistakes people make with strangers and casual acquaintances are simply thoughtless, occurring because they acted too quickly or assumed too much. To avoid those sorts of slipups, try to slow down, look around, and really pay attention to the people around you. You may find yourself needing to apologize less frequently.

CHAPTER 10

Public Apologies

Never make a defense or apology before you are accused.

—CHARLES I OF ENGLAND

The previous chapters have focused predominantly on apologies between individuals. However, the advent of worldwide telecommunications has created a community of public figures—actors, athletes, and other celebrities—with whom the general public feels a personal connection. Local shops and service providers have, in all too many instances, been replaced by huge corporations whose actions can impact whole societies. Politicians have always been accountable to their constituents, but these days a lawmaker's momentary lapse of judgment can quickly become an international scandal. We live in an age of public apologies, and a week rarely goes by when someone, somewhere, isn't making a statement apologizing to the public for something they've done wrong.

When a public figure or institution injures an individual, a private apology (as addressed in previous chapters) is essential, and an apology to the general public may also be in order. In fact, it's often necessary for public figures to be able to tell the world that they've privately apologized to the particular person or people most obviously injured by their actions. A simple statement of that fact usually isn't sufficient, though, because society at large has a separate relationship with its public figures and institutions, and that relationship also needs to be repaired when something goes awry.

Considering that most performers, athletes, politicians, and corporations have platoons of public relations experts at their beck and call, it's amazing how ineffective their public apologies often are. Fortunately, most of the mistakes that frequently mar public apologies are easy to avoid (see Chapter 15, "The Thirteen Most Common Ways to Botch an Apology"). Public apologies should always address the six essential elements of an effective apology (see Chapter 3), but apologizing to crowds rather than individuals can present additional special challenges. This chapter employs examples of famous public apologies to identify common stumbling blocks and offer suggestions on how to avoid them. While the advice offered in this chapter is likely to be helpful in crafting any public apology, there are certain public apology mistakes that are most commonly made by sports figures, performers, politicians, and companies, so each is addressed separately, respectively, below.

Public Apologies by Sports Figures

When athletes feel the need to make public apologies, it's frequently because they've used performance-enhancing drugs in violation of the rules of their sport, bet on games, or exhibited bad sportsmanship while playing. Off the playing field, they can incur the public's ire by abusing drugs or alcohol, indulging in sexual shenanigans that parents don't want to explain to their children, making obnoxious statements, or engaging in unsavory activities (such as dog fighting). Naïvely or not, Americans generally want to believe that their sports heroes are naturally gifted athletes, good sports, and, in their private lives, outstanding role models for the kids who worship them. When they learn otherwise, they're understandably disappointed.

If you're an athlete who has made a mistake and needs to make a public apology, there are some things to keep in mind as you prepare to do so.

Don't dally. It may be tempting to think that public outrage over your mistake will just blow over. If anything, it's more likely to swell to hurricane force the longer you wait to apologize. For example, after Cincinnati Reds star-player-turned-manager Pete Rose was accused of betting on baseball, he procrastinated for years, in fact decades, before he finally came clean and apologized. By the time the Reds celebrated the twenty-fifth anniversary of Rose's record-breaking 4,192nd hit, his tear-soaked apology for disrespecting the game, given at a roast in his honor, was a classic case of "too little, too late." Rose's refusal to admit wrongdoing didn't help him; he was banned from Major League Baseball for life, and many fans despise him for refusing to own up as much as for his original infraction. We'll never know whether coming clean right away would have resulted in the same outcome for Rose's career, but it seems likely that things would have come out more favorably for him if he'd been more immediately straightforward.

But before you rush to the microphones, if your mistake could land you in jail or other legal trouble, make sure your lawyer is involved in crafting your apology. Your statement should minimize the risk of your accidentally saying something you shouldn't, while still allowing you to say as much as you can as quickly as possible. In general, however, your fans will be much more likely to accept that your apology is sincere if it comes sooner rather than later.

Use your own voice. Nobody's good at everything, so it's not surprising if your skills as a public speaker aren't equal to your athletic prowess. The good news is that your fans won't expect you to be eloquent. They just want you to be sincere, and they'll believe more readily in your sincerity if you sound like yourself when you apologize. It's hard to imagine a more wooden public apology than the one Tiger Woods delivered months after it was discovered that he had cheated on his wife with dozens of women. He was clearly reading from a script that had been prepared for him by someone else, and his unwillingness or inability to face the camera and take questions didn't help matters at all. Woods returned to golf a notably diminished figure, stripped of many endorsement deals. The public has been reluctant to forgive him, and his obviously rehearsed statement remains a mark against him in the minds of many. Recognizing you're an athlete, not a speaker, your public relations experts will probably insist that you apologize from a prepared statement. Your job is to make sure it's written to sound like you (not like some slick PR guru's words have been put in your mouth), so you can deliver it with directness and sincerity.

Community service is good. You can't make personal amends to every one of your disappointed fans, but you can demonstrate your good faith through service to the greater good. After football superstar Michael Vick was indicted on various charges, including animal abuse, for his participation in dog fighting, he issued a public apology for his actions, but didn't stop there. Vick went on to partner with the Humane Society to speak out against cruelty to animals. You too can use your high-profile status to contribute to making the world a better place—in the process, such actions will help you make amends for your own mistakes.

Public Apologies by Performers

When performers need to make public apologies, it's usually because they've disappointed their fans by abusing drugs or alcohol, cheating on their spouses, or making offensive statements. Unlike professional athletes, performers can often appear very credible when they make public apologies, because communicating is their business, and they thrive in front of the camera. Actors and musicians are also less likely than sports heroes to be expected to be superb role models (unless they've been portrayed as living saints—we'll discuss that problem below). Still, performers also face certain common pitfalls that can be avoided with a little thought and care.

Pick a forgiving venue. Late-night talk-show host Jay Leno seems to have become the confessor of choice for performers who need to make public apologies, especially since Oprah Winfrey has moved on to other ventures. In one instance, Leno proved to be the perfect sympathetic ear when actor Hugh Grant apologized charmingly for having been caught dallying with a prostitute. If you haven't made it to Leno's call list, try to find a similarly comfortable setting from which to tell your fans how sorry you are.

Don't chew the scenery. While performers are typically much better than athletes at delivering public apologies, there's usually a risk that their enviable expressiveness will escalate into self-centered melodrama. For example, hip-hop superstar Kanye West was roundly criticized when he interrupted award winner Taylor Swift's acceptance speech at the 2009 MTV Video Music Awards to praise another of the nominees. Thereafter, West delivered hand-wringing apologies online, on Jay Leno's show, to Swift herself, and in a series of tweets that, taken together, amounted to pure overkill. When you need to make a public apology, do it well once or twice, then stop. Going overboard will only suggest to your audience that you're more concerned about your own public image than in making things right with whomever you have harmed.

The holier you seem, the harder you'll fall. Some performers become permanently entwined in the public's imagination with their most famous roles. For instance, no matter how many other roles he has played, Leonard Nimoy will always be identified with the enigmatic Mr. Spock of *Star Trek*, and Daniel Radcliffe may never be fully parted from his alter ego, Harry Potter. If a performer comes to be perceived by the public as saintly or straitlaced, she can expect her fans to be especially disappointed when her all-too-human failings are revealed. So, for example, when Martha Stewart was jailed for securities fraud and other charges, her crimes were particularly distressing to the fans of *Martha Stewart Living*, because they contrasted so sharply with their image of America's perfect homemaker. If your success as a performer has been based on an exceptionally wholesome image, or if you've specialized in entertaining children or members of a particular faith or even a particularly devoted fan base, recognize that your transgressions may seem more shocking than they would have if your image had been less pristine. Having been put on a pedestal, you'll have that much farther to fall and, consequently, that much farther to climb to redeem yourself. Be especially careful not to seem arrogant or defensive when you apologize, and expect to have to work harder than someone with a naughtier image would to get back in your fans' good graces.

Public Apologies by Politicians

Political satirist Mark Russell famously quipped that when it comes to ethical lapses, "with Republicans it's always money, and with the Democrats it's always sex." Recent news headlines suggest, however, that both sides of the aisle have engaged in scandals of both sorts, and probably will continue to do so as long as governments are run by human beings. Politicians most often get into trouble by taking improper campaign contributions or accepting bribes from powerful individuals or interest groups, engaging in various types of underhanded political deal-making, indulging in extramarital affairs or other inappropriate sexual antics, and drug- or alcohol-induced misconduct. When discovered, any of those misdeeds may require an apology not only to the individuals involved but also to the politician's colleagues and constituents.

The good news for politicians is that no one expects them, with very few exceptions, to be saints or role models, so it's rarely a shock when a politician does something that requires a public apology. The bad news is that politicians become powerful and prominent because they volunteer (indeed, campaign heroically) to lead the rest of us. Having sought to be raised above the masses, they can't really complain when they're held accountable for failing to live up to their campaign promises or widely held ethical standards.

No ifs, anys, or buts about it. For some reason, politicians seem especially prone to making conditional apologies, perhaps because their egos won't allow them to admit to wrongdoing. One classic example of an ineffective political apology came from former Senator Robert Packwood after he was accused of sexual assault, harassment, and abuse; Packwood responded with, "I'm apologizing for the conduct that it was alleged that I did." Not surprisingly, the press had a field day with Packwood's remarks, and his apology was a flop.

If you have to apologize to your constituents and the public, make sure your statements are completely devoid of the words *if* (as in, "I'm sorry *if* I offended anyone"), *any* (as in, "I'm sorry for *any* offense my actions may have caused"), or *but* (as in, "I'm sorry, but I had to do it for the sake of my poll numbers"). Assume you have offended—after all, that's why you're apologizing—and accept responsibility for whatever you did. (See also Chapter 15, "The Thirteen Most Common Ways to Botch an Apology.")

Tell the whole truth the first time. When former president Bill Clinton was first questioned about his relationship with White House intern Monica Lewinsky, he vigorously denied all wrongdoing—until the truth came out. By the time he finally admitted the full story, even his strongest supporters were furious with him, and his credibility was shot. When apologizing to your constituents and the public, don't wait to have the truth dragged out of you, and for heaven's sake, don't start by lying about what you have done. Recognize that the truth will eventually come out, and be honest enough to reveal it all yourself.

Don't blame the media. When former presidential hopeful Gary Hart challenged reporters to catch him in an extramarital affair, they did so in a matter of days. Hart apologized for his misdeeds, but then let loose with a tirade against the reporters who took up his challenge. While Hart had a point—reporters frequently appear to take particular pleasure in showing off politicians' shortcomings—the timing of his rant made it sound suspiciously like an excuse or deflection, or at least an excessive display of self-pity. Either way, it didn't set him up for a successful presidential run. Once you've chosen to run for public office, taking responsibility for your actions includes refraining from pointing fingers at the people who make them public.

Let your spouse stay home. There are countless examples of politicians from both sides of the aisle making public apologies with their spouses—usually wives—standing staunchly at their sides. The politician's hope may be to demonstrate that his wife has forgiven him, so the voters should, too. However, the sight of a tired, unhappy woman standing silently next to a man who has publicly humiliated her is far from inspiring, and may backfire with voters who decide that the wife is there solely for political reasons. If your wife or husband wants to stand with you during a public apology, accept the support as a gracious gift. But if that support is halfhearted or, worse, demanded by your campaign advisors, don't insist. Make your public apology by yourself, and work on healing any rifts in your marriage in private.

Public Apologies by Corporations

When giant companies make mistakes, they can impact people

around the globe. Product defects, financial misdeeds, and environmental accidents are among the most common reasons corporations have to apologize not only to individual consumers but sometimes to millions. Corporations survive, after all, on the strength of their customer relationships and public reputations. Consequently, a corporation's public apology has to be effective if its business is to survive a major error. If your business has to issue a public apology, there are some important things to consider.

Make the apology a priority. Corporations exist to make money by selling goods and services. Consequently, top executives frequently make the mistake of deferring public apologies while they grapple with the financial consequences of a major error. That mistake can be compounded when corporate counsel gets involved and wants to thoroughly examine every aspect of a mistake, which can take days or even weeks. Meanwhile, the company is being tried in the court of public opinion, and its silence may be taken for defensiveness or, worse, a lack of concern. If your company has made a mistake that seems likely to call for a public apology, put aside your other business and get your team going so you can issue that apology as quickly as possible.

Choose your spokesperson with care. When big companies issue public apologies, they need an individual to deliver the message, even if scores of people are working behind the scenes to help. Frequently, the president or chief executive officer of the company steps into that role, but he or she may not be the best choice. For example, when an oil rig operated by British Petroleum exploded in 2010, pouring millions of gallons of unrefined crude into the Gulf of Mexico, then-CEO Tony Hayward quickly issued a statement taking responsibility for the accident on his company's behalf. It was a good first step, but as efforts to cap the well failed and the oil continued to flow,

Hayward became short-tempered and abrupt. His seeming arrogance was offensive to everyone from residents of the Gulf whose lives had been forever altered by the spill to government officials who were working to contain it, and BP's efforts to maintain good public relations faltered. Ultimately, Hayward was replaced by Robert Dudley, first as BP's spokesperson and later as CEO.

Make (cautious) use of the Internet. Although emailed apologies can be disastrous between individuals, the Internet can be invaluable for corporations that need ready access to consumers around the world. Corporate blogs, Facebook, YouTube, and even Twitter provide excellent platforms for public apologies. In 2010, when questions arose concerning the safety of its automobiles, Toyota posted a carefully worded apology on YouTube that also ran as a television commercial. The automaker admitted that it had failed to pay sufficient attention to product safety and promised to work hard to regain consumers' trust. Although the piece might not have been sufficient alone, it proved to be an excellent contribution to Toyota's campaign to restore its brand.

Carefully (!) consider humor. It's usually not a good idea to use jokes in an apology, but when a mistake is relatively minor and the topic is right, humor at its own expense can make a corporation's apology more effective. In one famous example, Domino's Pizza, responding to criticism by customers for producing a less-than-delicious product, overhauled its pizza recipe, and then issued a series of tongue-in-cheek ads on television and the Internet, apologizing for its formerly inferior pizza and explaining what the company had done to make it more appetizing. The ads entertained consumers and encouraged them to give Domino's another try.

In spite of that success story, it's important to think carefully before injecting humor into a corporate apology. If Domino's had been apologizing for something more serious—for example, a food safety issue—joking around would have been a big mistake.

*   *   *   *

As with apologies in private settings, public apologies are all about restoring trust. The public is eager to think well of its athletes, entertainers, and elected officials, and wants to be able to rely on the companies that provide essential products and services. Effective apologies can help public figures and major corporations maintain great relationships with the millions of people they serve.

CHAPTER 11

How to Ask for an Apology

If you don't ask, you don't get.

—MAHATMA GANDHI

Up to this point, we've focused our discussions of apologies primarily on the person making the apology. However, there are at least two parties to every apology: the person making it and the person receiving it. If you're on the receiving end, you may have questions about how you can best accept an apology when it's offered (for that, see the next chapter). But what should you do when you believe you deserve an apology but have not received one? That depends on the particular circumstances. You might choose to let it go, but doing so may leave you feeling resentful, which can do lasting damage to your relationship with the other person. If you think that's a significant risk, you might be wise to ask for an apology.

Some people refuse to ask for apologies, based on the assumption, "If I have to ask, it won't be sincere." If that's your opinion, please reconsider. As you probably know from your own mistakes, it's easy to step on someone else's toes without realizing that you've done so. You can probably also remember times when you were so ashamed of what you did to someone else that you didn't apologize even though you probably should have. You know how your own apology slipups have affected your relationships, and you can probably think of at least one instance when you wish someone had asked for an apology from you instead of letting bad feelings fester. Do the other person the favor you wish someone had done for you, and ask for an apology when you think you deserve one. It will give you both a chance to clear the air and to restore good feelings between you.

Getting Ready

Once you decide to ask for an apology, there are some steps you should take before you approach the other person. Just as preparation can make an apology more effective, it can also make a request for an apology more likely to succeed, so take the time to consider the following questions.

Why do you want an apology? If you're asking for the apology because you want to mend fences and restore your relationship with the other person, great! If you want an apology because you think you deserve it and you want to put an upsetting incident behind you before leaving a relationship, that's okay, too. You might even want an apology to please someone else. For example, suppose you were out to dinner with your family, and the waiter made a snotty comment about kids in fancy restaurants. It didn't particularly offend you, but your son was upset. You might ask for an apology not for yourself, but because your son was reluctant to speak for himself.

Those are all good reasons to ask for an apology. But if you want an apology just to humiliate the person who offended you or to even a score, please think again. Apologies really should be about healing and reconciliation, not about making painful situations even more so. Take a little time and see if you can't bring yourself around to a more conciliatory state of mind before asking for an apology. Not only will you be more likely to receive one, the apology will be much more likely to satisfy you when you eventually receive it.

What are you really upset about? Just as it's harder to apologize effectively when you don't know what you've done wrong, it's harder to ask for an apology if you don't know what offended you. Imagine, for example, that your longtime sweetheart gave you a really practical, unromantic gift for Valentine's Day. You're unhappy about it and want him to apologize. Before you ask, though, consider what's really bothering you. Are you upset by the gift itself, or by your sense that he's less committed to you than you would like him to be? If the real problem is that you're ready to take your relationship to the next level and he isn't, no apology about the gift is likely to address what is really making you unhappy.

What will it take to make things right? If you're upset enough to ask for an apology, there's probably something you'd like the other person to do to make amends. It's usually a good idea to figure out what that might be prior to asking for the apology. Even if the other person isn't willing to give you exactly what you want, you'll be in a better position to agree on what might be enough to wipe the slate clean. For example, imagine your daughter borrowed your favorite sweater (again) and spilled something on it before returning it to your closet without saying anything about it. You might want her to pay for dry cleaning the sweater, in addition to grounding her for a week, and she might think that combination of penalties is too severe. Even if you're not going to pull rank and insist that she accept the punishment you have selected, you will be in a better position to agree on how she can make amends if you have already thought through what an appropriate penalty might be.

Deciding in advance on what you want the other person to do to make amends can also help you identify any absolute deal breakers that you must have for the apology to be effective. Suppose, for example, your husband has a history of repeatedly running up credit card bills that puts your family's financial security in danger, and he has done it again. While you are waiting for him to apologize to you, yet another outrageous Visa bill comes in. Thinking about it, you may also realize that you're entirely fed up with his financial irresponsibility, and what you really want him to do is relinquish all of his credit cards. If that's the only thing that will satisfy you, it's just as well to know it going into your conversation with him.

Do you owe an apology, too? In many situations, there is blame on both sides, and you may need to apologize to the person you're asking to apologize to you. It's normally a good idea to at least ask yourself whether you're partly responsible for the situation, for two reasons. First, if you haven't thought about it beforehand, and the other person points out where you were at fault, you'll be more likely to get defensive and make it even harder for the two of you to put things right. Second, if you know you owe the other person an apology, you can prepare for it and approach him or her with a little more humility, which increases the likelihood that your conversation will come to a good result.

Where and how will you ask? In the same way that you would think about when and where to offer an apology, you should consider your time, place, and medium for asking for one. If it's a bad idea to apologize electronically (and it almost always is), it's usually even worse to ask for an apology by email or text message. The person receiving your request may read more into the request than you intended and get defensive, which won't help relations between you at all. As with giving apologies, a request for an apology is usually best delivered face-to-face or, if that's impractical, by telephone. Select a time when you and the other person will be able to talk as long as necessary. And consider how you'll gracefully exit the conversation once your request for an apology has been addressed.

Asking for the Apology

Once you're ready to ask for the apology, you may be a little nervous. Don't be too worried about getting it wrong. After all, you're the one who is owed an apology, and you're being gracious enough to ask for it instead of holding a grudge. Here are some tips on how to make your request as successful as possible.

Be calm and direct. If you're extremely emotional when you ask for an apology, the other person may get emotional too, and it will be more difficult for the two of you to talk things through. Asking for an apology can be a little touchy, and the calmer you are, the less likely it is that the other person will get defensive and upset. It's also a good idea to simply say, "I would like an apology from you." If you beat around the bush or start waffling, you may confuse the other person. Please note that it's probably not a good idea to say, "You owe me an apology." While it may be true, the other person may hear "you owe me" as an attack, whereas "I would like" may sound less confrontational.

Tell your side of the story. The fifth essential element of an effective apology is to listen to the person receiving it, so you have every reason to expect the apology to include an opportunity for you to explain why you were offended. Just remember, though, that the person who is going to apologize to you can't listen if you don't talk. You may be reluctant to open up about what upset you enough to drive you to request an apology, but there are three good reasons to do so.

First, the other person may not have considered your human vulnerabilities, so opening up creates the opportunity for better understanding between you. Returning to the example of the stained sweater, your daughter may not realize that you feel helpless and even a little violated when she takes things you treasure and damages them; helping her recognize that you have feelings too will strengthen your relationship in the long run.

Second, if you don't tell the other person what you think happened and how you felt about it, you may find later that you're still carrying some lingering resentments that can undermine your relationship. Let's say, for example, that your boss made a comment about how "lucky" you were to win an important contract from your competitors after protracted bidding. If you don't politely point out that the contract award was actually the product of a lot of hard, thoughtful work, your boss may continue to believe that you're more lucky than smart. That probably isn't what you want him or her to think, and you're likely to become increasingly resentful if you don't straighten things out. Or, to use a more personal example, imagine that your husband spent a family afternoon at the beach ignoring you while ogling pretty girls in skimpy swimsuits. You could swallow hard and say nothing, but you might be hard-pressed not to give him the "silent but resentful" treatment later.

Third, if the other person doesn't know what you experienced and how you felt about it, he or she may be more likely to make the same mistake with you in the future. For example, suppose your assistant made a thoughtless remark about how disorganized you are when he happened to be talking to your boss. Unless you tell him that his comment was hurtful and offensive, he may make similar jokes in the future, damaging your credibility in the office and your future working relationships. The same would hold true if your husband makes a snide comment to your friends next door about how tough it is to get you to do your share around the house. If you don't tell him that you thought his remarks were far from funny he may do it again, hurting your feelings and potentially damaging your relationship.

Apologize first. If you think you owe the other person an apology, deliver it before you ask for one in return. Your apology may clear the air between you and make it easier for the other person to reciprocate. But don't indulge in an "I'm sorry for what I did, but I wouldn't have done X if you hadn't said Y" pseudo-apology, because you'll only make matters worse. Deliver your own apology as if you weren't going to ask for one in return, and take responsibility for your own actions instead of blaming the other person for what you did wrong.

Express your gratitude. Whether you get your apology or not (and if you don't, read on), thank the other person for letting you have your say. While it can be difficult to ask for an apology, it may be even tougher to be asked. Not only is the person hearing that he did something that upset you enough that you want an apology, he also has to absorb the implication that he was too clueless to recognize that he'd made a mistake in the first place. Thanking the other person for listening is the courteous thing to do, even if he doesn't give you an apology.

When the Other Person Refuses to Apologize

Most people want to do the right thing most of the time. That means you'll probably get a sincere apology from almost everyone you ask. (If you aren't sure how to accept the apology, check out Chapter 12.) Once in a great while, though, someone will refuse outright to apologize. When that happens, the following steps might be of help.

Politely leave the room. Once someone has refused to apologize to you, the odds that a tense conversation will escalate into a full-blown battle increase dramatically. Your job, at that point, is to get out of the conversation and, if you're face-to-face, out of the room without contributing to an escalation in hostilities. Thank the other person for her time, and leave without saying anything else to offend her. Once you're alone in a quiet place, you can consider your next steps.

Review the conversation. While it's not usually a good idea to rumi-
nate endlessly on an upsetting conversation, it can be beneficial to
think back once or twice on what led the other person to refuse to
apologize. Did you say or do something offensive when you asked for
the apology? Was the timing of your request bad? Is the other person
naturally so proud or defensive that she'll refuse to apologize even
when it's perfectly obvious that she should? Is your relationship so
unequal that she simply won't to apologize to you? (As we discussed
in Chapter 6, "Apologies in the Workplace," some people don't ever
apologize to those they consider subordinates because they think it
makes them look weak.) Does the other person have a completely different perspective on what happened between you? Is the other
person afraid to admit to a mistake or to take responsibility for her
actions?

The purpose of reviewing the conversation is not to look for
reasons to be angry with the other person or to beat yourself up for
"doing it wrong." At this point, your goal is not to assign blame, but
to decide how to move forward. A request for an apology can't be
called back, so if your request is refused, you'll need to consider how
to deal with the other person and whether your relationship needs
to change.

Consider your options. If the person who refused to apologize to you
has a relatively unimportant role in your life, you may just want to
avoid engaging with him or her in the future. Salesclerks, waiters,
cabbies, and other casual business associates can usually be replaced
fairly easily, so you might choose not to frequent a particular shop,
restaurant, or other venue again once one of them has refused to apologize to you.

Then again, you may not want to give up a preferred locale just
because a particular employee was rude. If, for example, the arrogant
new salesclerk at your favorite wine shop sneered at your choice of

Chardonnay and laughed off your request for an apology, you might try a different tack than switching stores. Consider politely but firmly asking to speak to the manager, then describe to her what happened. You'll most likely get an apology from the manager, and the salesclerk will probably get a much-needed lesson in customer service.

Other business associates—your boss, your colleagues at work, key customers or clients, and professional service providers like your doctor, attorney, or accountant—may be difficult to avoid or replace. If one of them refuses to apologize, you'll have to consider carefully how much you value the relationship and just how important the requested apology really is to you. Especially if the relationship has been good over a significant period of time, you may decide to let the requested apology go undelivered. On the other hand, if you've had unpleasant encounters with this person before, it might be time to find a new job or switch to a new doctor.

If a cherished friend or family member refuses to apologize to you, your options may be more limited. Unless her refusal to apologize was the final straw, and you're ready to end the relationship, you'll need to find a way to reconcile. In these situations, time can be a great healer. Let a few hours or days go by, and then try to talk to your friend or family member again. You might not get an apology per se, but you may just get to a better mutual understanding.

Wait and watch. Sometimes people who aren't able or willing to get the words "I'm sorry" past their teeth will still try to make things right with you. If someone refuses to apologize to you, that doesn't mean he's not sorry for what he did or is uninterested in making things right with you. Watch the other person for the next few days and see whether he goes out of his way to do something nice for you. Your father, for instance, might not be willing to apologize for the unkind things he said to your boyfriend, but you might find that your household chores miraculously finish themselves for a few days. If so, you may decide to accept that good deed as a kind of apology, even though the words "I'm sorry" were never spoken.

*   *   *   *

Even if one request for an apology goes badly, don't let one person's refusal to apologize dissuade you from ever asking for an apology again. Keep the faith. No human interaction is foolproof, but as Mahatma Gandhi said, "If you don't ask, you don't get." Asking for an apology may feel risky, but it beats stewing in aggrieved silence almost every time.

CHAPTER 12

How to Accept an Apology

We are all full of weakness and errors;
let us mutually pardon each other our follies.

—Voltaire

The people around you are human, and will make mistakes from time
to time the same way you will. When someone's actions harm or
offend you, you may find yourself receiving an apology, maybe even
one you have asked for. You will go a long way toward healing your
relationship with the person who wronged you simply by accepting
the apology gracefully.

The Basics of Accepting an Apology

The how-tos for accepting an apology are similar to those for giving
an apology. As you'll see, accepting an apology can involve much of
the same advance planning as giving one, and the essential elements
of an effective apology are mirrored in an effective acceptance.
Ultimately, both parties' goal should be to mend fences and restore
good relations. The better your acceptance, the more likely that goal is
to be met. So if someone tells you they owe you an apology, think
about these points before you sit down to talk.

Find the right time and place. If you have the opportunity to do so,
schedule the apology for a time and place that's mutually convenient.
For example, imagine that your best friend has been out of touch for
months, then suddenly texts a message saying, "I've been neglecting

you—can we talk?" If you've been feeling hurt and angry, don't immediately call her. You'll be less receptive to her apology, and the odds are good that your conversation won't go well. Instead, text back (one of the few times a text can be a useful tool when making or receiving apologies) and suggest a couple of times and locations where you can comfortably talk things out.

This technique can work even if the person offering you an apology is right in front of you. For example, let's say your husband wants to apologize to you for making a sarcastic comment about the meal you just cooked, and starts apologizing while you're putting your children to bed. There's nothing wrong with asking him to wait a few minutes until you can give each other your full attention, and there's a much better chance his apology will lead to reconciliation if you do.

Listen carefully. If someone is apologizing to you, the odds are pretty good that you're at least a little angry with him or her. Anger can be tremendously distracting, and can make it difficult for you to listen to the other person as he or she apologizes. Unless you've decided to write that person off once and for all, however, you'll need to make yourself calm down enough to really hear what's being said. If you don't, you're likely to miss or misinterpret something important the other person says, wasting an opportunity to understand what happened better. Or you may wonder later why he or she left it out, which can make you angry all over again. Either way, your failure to listen can ruin the apology and put your relationship back in jeopardy. If you pay full attention the first time, both of you will benefit.

Resist the temptation to listen with half an ear while thinking about what you're going to say in response. People can be so concerned about their part in a difficult conversation that they spend the entire time rehearsing their responses and miss what the other person has to say. Don't worry about how well you're going to explain your side of things. After all, you're the wronged party or you wouldn't be receiving an apology. That means you deserve some latitude in how you reply.

Careful listening can help you make sure that the person apologizing to you understands fully what went wrong and why you're upset about it. Imagine that your teenage son borrowed your car without permission, drove the gas tank dry, left the interior covered in junk food wrappers, and came home after curfew. Say he apologizes only for the empty tank and the mess inside, because he doesn't realize that you're concerned less about the state of your car than about his safety driving late and about the disrespect he showed you by taking the car without asking permission in the first place. Unless you listen with your full attention while he apologizes, you may miss the opportunity to set the record straight, and give your son a valuable lesson.

Listening carefully will also allow you to make a better on-the-spot assessment of how sincere the other person's apology really is. Remember, sincerity is the most essential element of an effective apology, so if you ultimately conclude that the other person has been insincere, you're likely to be offended all over again. If you don't listen carefully, you may come to that conclusion in error, and then the mistake will be yours. Give the other person your full attention, and you'll be better able to assess whether the apology is genuine.

Reciprocate if you should. While in some situations there may be one wrongdoer and one victim, frequently both parties are at least somewhat to blame when an apology is in order. Let's say, for example, that a colleague embarrassed you in a meeting in front of your boss, and you responded by chewing her out as soon as the meeting was over. Your colleague shouldn't have spoken so thoughtlessly, but you probably shouldn't have lost your temper, either. If she was gracious enough to apologize first for embarrassing you, be equally gracious and apologize in return. Even if you're still angry with her, apologizing for your own mistake will help you start making things right and, ultimately, strengthen your professional relationship.

Similarly, let's say that during a phone call your mother started complaining yet again about a time you misbehaved and embarrassed her when you were thirteen years old. (Assume that at least ten years have gone by since the incident in question.) You hung up on her, tired of being berated for an ancient offense that you can't remedy now. She shouldn't have brought the incident up again, but you shouldn't have hung up on her, either. When she calls back to apologize, tell her you're sorry, too.

Talk it through. One of the essential elements of an effective apology is letting the person you've offended tell his or her side of the story. As the person receiving an apology, you'll help make that apology more effective if you tell the other person what happened from your perspective, how you felt about it, and why you were hurt or offended. Don't be surprised if your respective takes on the situation are very different.

Stay as calm as you can when explaining your perspective, and don't let the other person interrupt. There will be plenty of time for dialogue once you've gotten your version of things on the table. If you can, put aside the assumption that the other person hurt or offended you deliberately, and don't accuse him or her of dishonesty or malice. Angry accusations aren't likely to lead to reconciliation. At the same time, don't minimize your own feelings or start making excuses for the other person's behavior. If you do, you're likely to come away from the conversation still angry with him or her and annoyed with yourself for not being more assertive.

Telling the other person what you saw and felt will help him or her avoid the inclination to minimize what he or she did. You already know from the times when you've had to apologize how difficult it can be and how tempting it is to pretend that what you did wasn't "all that bad." For example, imagine your father started telling your fiancé how fat you were as a child, ignoring the emotional scars you still carry into adulthood, even though you've worked hard to slim down. If you don't tell him how painful his comments are, he'll be able to pretend that he did nothing more than fondly reminisce about his once-little girl.

There are two more good reasons to tell your side of the story. First, if you don't tell the other person what you think happened and how you felt about it, you may find later that you're still carrying some lingering resentments that can undermine your relationship. For example, imagine that a friend borrowed some antique tools you inherited from your grandfather and six months later still hadn't returned them. When you finally called and asked for them back, he brought them by and offered a halfhearted apology, clearly not understanding why getting them back is such a big deal to you. If you don't tell your friend that you were upset by his carelessness and explain why the tools are so important to you, he may come away thinking you're too persnickety, and you may find yourself fuming later because he was so cavalier about a family treasure. Neither will be good for your friendship.

Second, if the other person doesn't know what you experienced and how you felt about it, he or she may be more likely to make the same mistake with you in the future. Let's say, for instance, that your babysitter let your children watch a violent movie on television. You called her on it, and she apologized but didn't seem to quite understand why you were so upset. If you don't explain to her that you find the whole idea of violence as entertainment morally repugnant and that you feel that she seriously violated your trust, she may not realize that, for you, letting the kids watch a horror flick is a really big deal. She may do it again after a time or two, and your relationship with her will suffer at best, and end at worst.

Telling the other person what you think happened and how you felt about it can be particularly important if this isn't the first time the other person has made a particular mistake. For example, suppose your boss frequently drops by your office as you're about to leave at the end of the workday for a "short" discussion that makes you late getting home. When your boss apologizes for keeping you late for the third or fourth time, you're probably wise to politely point out that he's kept you late several times before and that the delay creates significant problems for you. You may find out in the ensuing discussion that your boss thinks you haven't been working hard enough or that he doesn't respect your time enough to care when you get to leave in the evening. That may not be good news, but it's probably something you ought to know. If, on the other hand, your boss honestly doesn't realize how often he keeps you late, pointing out that a pattern has developed can help him be more sensitive to your time constraints.

After you've had your say, listen again. The other person will undoubtedly want to further explain his or her side of the story, and you'll end up on better terms with one another if you've both had your say. Think of the conversation as being like a game of tennis, in which the players start out lobbing the ball back and forth from twenty feet apart, and end up shaking hands over the net. Each return of the ball brings you and the other person a little closer to a mutual understanding.

Express your gratitude. Even if the other person's apology was late, badly delivered, or incomplete, he or she at least made an attempt at it. Regardless of what you may think of how the apology was delivered, thank the other person for making the effort. You've had to make apologies, too, so you know how difficult it is. Thanking the other person is the gracious thing to do, and it will make the apology more effective for you both.

Forgive if you can. Once the other person has apologized and you've talked the matter through, forgive the other person as best you can.

Yes, he or she made a mistake, but we all do. The other person probably isn't an irredeemable monster—he or she is probably just another fallible human being who stumbled. While you may find it difficult to forgive, doing so has several advantages.

First, the other person may be someone with whom you'll have to continue to interact. For example, let's say that one of your more ambitious colleagues, Paul, took credit for one of your better ideas with your mutual boss. Paul later apologized to you and went to your boss to explain what happened and make sure your boss knew that the great idea was yours and not his. At that point, Paul has pretty much done all he can to make things right with you. Unless you want to quit your job and go to another company where everyone is perfect (good luck with that), you're going to have to deal with Paul every workday. You don't have to become Paul's best friend, and you're probably wise to be a little more cautious with him after that incident, but refusing to forgive him won't improve matters and may seriously hamper your ability to work with him in the future.

Second, if you forgive Paul, you'll earn points with your boss and other people in the office for your maturity. Clinging to a grudge against Paul will eventually make you appear childish and petty. Even if your boss completely agrees with you that Paul was out of line, unless she fires him you have to assume that she expects you to forgive him and get on with business. She's undoubtedly far more interested in meeting the company's goals than in refereeing fights between her staff members. The same goes for other people in the office. Even if they know what Paul did and completely agree that he was out of line, they'll eventually lose patience with you if you continue to hold a grudge against him. Do your boss and your co-workers a favor, forgive Paul, and get back to work.

Third, forgiving Paul will relieve you of a tremendous internal burden. Life is short and far too precious to travel through loaded down with grudges. If you don't forgive Paul, every hour you spend dealing with him will be unpleasant for you and you'll probably end up feeling a lot more miserable about it than he will. As one wise person put it, "Resentment is like a glass of poison that a man drinks, then he sits down and waits for his enemy to die." Don't poison yourself with unresolved resentment—put the glass down by forgiving.

Forgiving other people has one other advantage. Even when you're really offended by something another person has done to you, you've made mistakes in the past and will make them in the future. If you start characterizing other people's mistakes as "unforgivable," sooner or later you're going to start thinking the same way about your own shortcomings—and so will others. By contrast, if you make it a point to forgive other people for the things they do to hurt and offend you, you'll find it easier to forgive yourself when you do something you wish you hadn't. They will also find it easier to forgive you in the future.

Reconcile if you wish. People frequently make the mistake of thinking that forgiving someone requires you to go back to the exact same relationship you had with that person. That's not only untrue, it's probably impossible. Every experience you have with another person shapes your relationship going forward, and it's rarely wise to ignore your feelings when dealing with other people. Even if you've forgiven another person, your level of trust and respect for him or her may have been diminished. Don't try to force yourself to "feel better" about that person. Respect your feelings, and let your perception of him or her improve over time if it's going to do so.

It's also important to respond to the lessons that you learn about other people when they injure you. Using the previous example, Paul's actions have taught you that Paul may be tempted to steal your ideas again if his ambition gets out of control. You needn't be hostile with Paul going forward, but that doesn't mean you should be as trusting with him as you were before. Forgive him, be pleasant to him, but don't share any more ideas with him unless you don't care if he claims them for his own. As the ancient Chinese proverb says, "Fool me once, shame on you—fool me twice, shame on me." Don't give Paul another opportunity to profit at your expense until time and experience demonstrate that he has learned his lesson.

Don't harbor a secret grudge. While you aren't obliged to return to the same relationship you had with someone just because she apologized do you, it's disingenuous at best to pretend to accept an apology while continuing to seethe inside. If you can't accept an apology, or can't bring yourself to return to your prior relationship, be honest about it. You're allowed to be human and to struggle with mixed emotions. But if you covertly hang onto hard feelings after saying you've accepted someone's apology, it'll only be a matter of time before you say or do something hurtful. You'll be embarrassed, the other person will feel betrayed, and your relationship will suffer even more. Once you say "apology accepted," be prepared to let the bad feelings go.

Accepting Problem Apologies

Some circumstances can make it particularly difficult to accept an apology. Perhaps the other person hurt you especially badly, or has offended you so many times that yet another apology from him or her just isn't credible any more. Perhaps you're still too offended to have a meaningful discussion, or your feelings about that person have reached the point where you just can't face going back into a relationship with him or her. (For more on such situations, see the next section of the book, "Problem Apologies.") When accepting an apology is particularly tough, there are some things to keep in mind that may make it go more smoothly.

Delay if you must. If the other person made a really serious mistake, and you're still far too offended or upset to discuss the situation, tell him or her that you need some time to calm down before you'll be ready to talk. For example, suppose you learned that a co-worker had been spreading lies about you in the office in order to beat you out for a promotion. You have every right in that situation to be upset. If your co-worker heard that you knew about the slander and came to you to apologize, chances are good that you'd lose your temper and make matters worse. Say something like, "I appreciate your coming to me, but I'm not ready to discuss what you did just yet. Give me a few days to settle down, and then we can talk." That's not only acceptable, it's probably a very good idea, if you want to keep your composure when you and the other person finally talk.

Once you've put the discussion off, though, don't delay forever. The longer you wait to talk with the other person, the harder it will start to seem, and the more likely it will be that you'll never have the conversation at all. You won't get your apology, the other person won't get a chance to be forgiven, and your relationship will be damaged beyond repair. Here's an example of just such a situation:

Donna and Karen were co-workers who, over the course of a few years, became good friends. Karen was intelligent and witty, and Donna enjoyed her company so much that she tended to overlook the fairly significant differences in their personal values. When Karen's pointed wit offended other people in the office, Donna stuck up for her, and when Karen started borrowing money, supplies, files, and other small items from her co-workers, Donna chalked up Karen's failure to return them to forgetfulness. Matters came to a head when Karen, who seemed to be chronically short of money, borrowed several hundred dollars from Donna for repairs to her car, and never repaid it. Six months later, Donna learned that Karen had again borrowed the same amount of money, allegedly to make the same repairs, from another co-worker, Evan, who was new to the office and unaware of Karen's habits. Donna confronted Karen, who claimed that the car had "broken down again," but Donna suddenly found herself feeling that Karen had been using her for years. When Karen approached her a few days later, behaving as though nothing had happened, Donna refused to let Karen explain or apologize, telling her, "I will be in touch when I'm ready to talk." The promised conversation never took place, and the friendship between Donna and Karen was never mended. Donna said later that although she didn't particularly want to continue as Karen's friend and confidante, she regretted never having explained to Karen why she was so angry. In hindsight, Donna also wished she had kept her promise because the incident left a loose end between her and Karen that made their dealings in the office awkward and uncomfortable, for them and for others.

Consider setting conditions. If you're reluctant to accept an apology until the person offering it makes amends, that's perfectly acceptable in some situations. Imagine, for example, that your friend Nina is a delightful but scatterbrained individual who frequently makes promises she doesn't keep. She coaxed you into lending her an expensive necklace to wear to a formal dinner and, sure enough, managed to break the clasp before returning it to you. Charmingly apologetic, Nina has promised to pay to have the necklace repaired to make amends. Depending on how many times Nina has burned you in the past and how upset you are by her latest mistake, you may not want to fully accept her apology until the necklace is fixed and back in your hands.

Examine your own actions. When it's particularly difficult to accept an apology, our own actions, expectations, and motivations are often critical factors. If you're struggling to accept an apology, you might want to ask yourself what's holding you back. Do you have unrealistic expectations of this person? Are you still angry about what happened, or about something else you haven't discussed? Are you letting personal pride get in the way? Is it more important to you to be right than to be in a relationship with this person? Are you refusing to accept the apology because you know you should apologize, too, and you don't want to do it? Are you afraid to accept the apology because of what someone else will think? If you take the time to look inward, you may be surprised at what you find. And if you decide, ultimately, that you simply can't remain in the relationship with the other person, read on.

Ending a Relationship

Even after you've forgiven someone, you may find that you don't want to stay in a relationship with him or her. That's your right—no relationship, whether business or personal, is a prison sentence, and it's usually better to leave a relationship than to stay if you're miserable. Here's an example of one situation in which forgiveness didn't lead to reconciliation:

Ann and Kelly had been business colleagues for years when their new boss, Carl, was hired. Although Ann and Kelly were on generally good terms with one another, their previous boss had favored Ann, and Kelly was jealous of Ann's past successes. Eager to impress their new boss, Kelly started talking to Carl behind Ann's back, belittling Ann's work and implying that Ann was lazy and none too bright. Carl couldn't help but be influenced by Kelly's comments, and he started ignoring Ann's recommendations and excluding her from important meetings. One of their co-workers overheard one of Kelly's conversations with Carl, and told Ann. Furious, Ann confronted Kelly, who admitted almost immediately what she had done and apologized sincerely to Ann. She explained that she was jealous of Ann, but admitted that she had gone about impressing Carl the wrong way. Ann was able to forgive Kelly and wish her well, but she was unwilling to reconcile with her. Ultimately, Ann decided to leave the company, accepting a position with another company, where she found a boss she could trust to talk to her directly instead of relying on gossip.

Calling it quits. Deciding to end a relationship is difficult, and you'll want to think carefully about the consequences. It's usually easier to exit a business relationship than a personal one, but even business relationships can be tough to leave. For example, imagine that you took your dog to your longtime veterinarian to have his teeth cleaned. When you picked up the dog, you discovered that the vet had pulled three teeth, including a canine, without asking you first. The bill was much higher than you expected, and you are unhappy that your dog will have to get by without a full set of teeth. You may decide never to return to your vet, or you may decide that the years of good service your pets have received outweigh this one incident. Before you make a final decision, there's nothing wrong with expressing displeasure, and you certainly should give your vet an opportunity to apologize and explain his choices.

Other people may try to dissuade you from leaving a relationship, particularly if you're giving up a lucrative job, a long-standing friendship, or a marriage (and you can almost count on opposition when there are children involved). Listen to their advice, weigh your options carefully, and consider consulting a professional counselor to help you sort out your feelings before you bring an important relationship to an end. But don't let social pressure force you to stay in a relationship that you truly wish or need to leave. For example, suppose your spouse has become abusive over the course of your marriage, but always apologizes extravagantly after every abusive incident, promising it will never happen again. There may be people who will pressure you to stay together "for the sake of the children," and even you, depending on your own background and expectations, may not recognize your spouse's ugly behavior to be truly abusive, especially if the abuse is verbal rather than physical. This little book can't tell you whether to stay in your marriage or not, but we urge you to get professional counseling if you're unsure. Outside advice from a trained expert can be essential in helping you make the critical decision of whether to stay or go.

Rethinking your approach. Sometimes people stay in difficult relationships for the sake of someone else, but it's possible to leave one relationship without destroying others. Let's say, for example, that your in-laws are constantly critical of you, and you've reached the point at which no apology from them, however heartfelt, would be enough to make you comfortable in their company. After talking things over with your spouse, you may conclude that the best thing you can do is to avoid seeing or speaking with them. That conclusion may not delight your spouse, but it needn't end your marriage, either. Let your spouse see them alone, and see if that doesn't take a significant burden off both of you.

You may also find that you're able to consider reconciliation after some time has passed or circumstances have changed. For example, your in-laws may be a lot more willing to be civil to you once there's a new grandchild in the picture. Stay flexible in your approach to your relationships, and you may find you can reconcile to at least some extent with a person who has injured you after some time has passed. Just knowing that you're free to leave a relationship may make it easier for you to stay in it, or to go back to it on your own terms.

Not Accepting an Apology

You can, of course, refuse to accept an apology. Doing so can have serious consequences, however, not only in your dealings with the other person but in your relationships with other people as well. While some people may see a refusal to accept an apology as a display of strength, most of us think that people who won't accept an apology are arrogant and rude. Even if you can't bring yourself to reconcile fully with someone who has injured you, accepting an apology and forgiving the other person usually will help you move forward and strengthen your relationships with other people who are aware of the injury that person inflicted on you. Being known as someone who graciously accepts apologies is great for your reputation and your relationships. It can also be good for your own peace of mind. Here's a situation in which accepting a difficult apology brought emotional healing to everyone involved:

Gabrielle was a lively young woman from a strictly religious family whose behavior didn't always comply with their church's tenets. Her grandmother, the family matriarch, continually criticized Gabrielle and ultimately expelled her "sinning" granddaughter from the family. For many years afterward, Gabrielle had limited contact with her parents and siblings, and almost none with her grandmother, and was deeply hurt by their rejection. It was only when her grandmother was diagnosed with cancer that the family permitted Gabrielle to return and help provide her grandmother with the intensive nursing care that she needed. On her deathbed, the grandmother took Gabrielle's hand and finally said, "I'm so sorry." Gabrielle accepted her apology, the old woman died in peace, and Gabrielle was able to forgive and begin a new, more mutually accepting relationship with the rest of her family.

* * * *

An apology, even one perfectly delivered, can go only so far, and most apologies are less than perfect. However, when an apology, even the clumsiest one, is accepted well, it can lead to healed and strengthened relationships. When someone offers you an apology, they're also offering you an opportunity to make peace. It's almost always a great idea to take it.

PART THREE

PROBLEM APOLOGIES

CHAPTER 13

Apologizing for a Serious Transgression

True remorse is never just a regret over
consequences; it is a regret over motive.

—Mignon McLaughlin

Some misdeeds are major. Murder, theft, assault, rape, child abuse, and adultery are all serious transgressions that will create lasting anger and hurt in the victims. While it would be wonderful if every bad act a person carried out could be instantly excused after an apology, some behavior is so atrocious that it may be unforgivable. For example, the Holocaust that resulted in the brutal murder of more than eleven million innocent people across Europe, six million of them Jews, has left an indelible stain on European history. Most people today were not even alive when the Holocaust occurred, but for many of us the Nazis are still the ultimate embodiment of evil, and it is almost impossible to imagine any apology that would be sufficient to repair the damage they did.

Individuals also commit seemingly unforgivable crimes. While their actions may be beyond forgiveness, that does not mean they shouldn't apologize. It's not uncommon for convicted criminals to issue public apologies to their victims and their families. While these apologies may seem self-serving (and some are, intended solely to avoid death sentences or extended jail terms), they can also help bring closure to the victims and offer the wrongdoer at least a little peace of mind.

In some cases, it's not the act itself that makes an action seem unforgivable but the motive or level of carelessness behind it. For example, if you accidentally injured a child who suddenly ran out into the street in front of your car, you might be able to apologize effectively to the child's parents for the injury, especially after a little time had passed. However, if you were speeding or driving drunk when you hit the child, it would be a lot harder to apologize effectively, because your carelessness was such a major contributing factor. If you deliberately ran the child down, apologizing effectively would be almost impossible, because your intent was nearly as bad as the act itself. You might apologize, but the child's parents would be unlikely to forgive you.

Even if forgiveness is a near impossibility, that doesn't mean you shouldn't try to make an apology. If you've done something seriously wrong, don't assume that any apology is too little or too late. Maybe you can't make things right, but you can still make them better.

Before You Issue an Apology

If you've done something really serious and you want to apologize, the best gift you can give to the victims or survivors is to take their feelings into consideration. Don't even think about apologizing before you take the following steps. Apologizing badly for a serious transgression can only make matters worse.

Figure out why you're apologizing. If you're apologizing just to evade or lessen the consequences of your offense, don't bother. Your efforts to avoid paying the price for your misconduct will only make you look worse. If, to use an awful example, you're convicted of murder, a halfhearted apology delivered through the press on the day of your sentencing won't fool anyone. Your "apology" will be recognized for exactly what it is—a self-serving effort to escape full punishment for your crime. Apologize because you did something wrong and are sincerely sorry for it, not because you hope that apologizing will help your situation.

Accept the penalty. If your actions were seriously wrong, there will be serious consequences, and making amends means taking your medicine. If, for example, you're caught embezzling funds from your company, you'll almost certainly be fired and you may face criminal charges. Don't accuse your company of making you a scapegoat or try to argue that the criminal charges are misplaced. Acknowledge your guilt, and accept that what you did was bad enough that you deserve to be punished for it.

Sometimes the penalty for doing something seriously wrong includes having to face the person you injured and listen to his or her description of the pain you caused. If, for example, you got a promotion at work by falsely claiming credit for your colleague Mark's hard work, Mark may have a lot to say to you when he finds out about your lies. Don't try to avoid that conversation—you can't apologize effectively to Mark or your company's management unless and until Mark has had his say.

The Apology

Once you are clear about why you want to apologize, and are ready to do so sincerely and to accept the consequences of your misdeed, you still need to tread very carefully with the apology. Here are some ways to avoid the most common pitfalls.

Don't deny your bad intent. If you deliberately did something wrong or hurtful to someone else, don't try to pretend it was an accident. Most of us like to think we're too good to be cruel, violent, or deceitful, but all of us are human, and we all have less-than-saintly moments from time to time. Pretending you didn't mean to hurt someone else is just another way of trying to avoid the consequences of your misconduct. To use the example of taking credit for Mark's work, don't pretend that you forgot who did what or that you didn't know what Mark did. Admit openly that you thought the work was so terrific that you claimed it for your own and that you shouldn't have done it. Your apology will be far more effective that way.

Don't demand forgiveness. When you've done something seriously wrong, apologizing for it is the least you can do. The person or people you've harmed may choose to forgive you if you apologize, but you're not entitled to forgiveness and an apology alone may not be enough to make things right. If, for example, you tried to rob an old woman and gave her a fatal heart attack in the process, your apology, however heartfelt, won't bring the woman back to her life and her loved ones. Forgiveness is a gift, not an entitlement. Consider yourself fortunate if you receive it, not cheated if you don't.

Don't stage a sideshow. We've all seen highly publicized cases in which convicted criminals have read their prepared apologies into banks of TV and radio microphones while the cameras flashed away. Apologizing in a media event may or may not make a favorable impression on the public as a whole, but it probably won't do anything to satisfy the people you injured. If, for example, you mismanaged your company's pension fund and cost the employees and their families their future financial security, those people probably won't get much satisfaction out of hearing your apology on CNN. Speak to the press if you must, but recognize that you probably need to apologize specifically to the people you injured as well, if you want your apology to be effective. (See Chapter 10, "Public Apologies," for more on handling such situations.)

*   *   *   *

Making an apology in any venue may be only the beginning of a long process to set things right. In Chapter 16, "After You Apologize," we'll look at some additional steps you may need to take after you apologize, to make your apology as effective as possible.

CHAPTER 14

Apologizing under Difficult Circumstances

*Our prime purpose in this life is to help others. And if
you can't help them, at least don't hurt them.*

—DALAI LAMA

Sometimes, no matter how careful or well intentioned you are, the
circumstances make it very difficult for you to apologize to someone
you've injured or offended. There are various reasons this might be
true, and each poses its unique challenges. When you find yourself in
one of the following situations in which an apology does not seem to
be an option, you'll fare better if you keep a few key points in mind.

You Don't Think You Owe an Apology

If someone is angry with you and, after thoroughly examining your
actions, you honestly don't believe you've done anything wrong, it can
be very difficult to bring yourself to apologize. Let's say, for example,
that one of your colleagues, Millie, was late bringing you information
that you needed in order to complete your company's quarterly financial report. This wasn't an isolated incident—despite constant protests
of good intentions, Millie has been late with the required information
almost every quarter, always claiming she is "too busy" to get the
information to you any sooner. This time, though, she was even later
than usual, forcing you to stay at the office long after hours and to
cancel a much-anticipated dinner date with a friend who was visiting

from out of town. When Millie finally brought the information to you, you angrily told her that you were tired of waiting for her and that you intended to complain to your mutual boss first thing the next morning. You made good on your threat, and the boss chewed Millie out. Now, everyone in the office knows that Millie is furious with you, and she snubs you every time you try to speak with her. At this point, you have several options.

Apologize anyway. Millie's chronic lateness has been an ongoing annoyance, and you had every right to ask her to be more prompt. Still, was it really necessary to get Millie in trouble with your boss, or were you just acting out of anger over missing your dinner date? If, after thinking carefully about it, you decide that you overreacted, apologize to Millie for doing so. You don't have to accept her constant lateness, but apologizing for having lost your temper may be a good way to open the door to a conversation about how to avoid similar problems in the future.

Express your feelings. If, after thinking about it, you honestly conclude that going to your boss was your only remaining alternative and that you weren't acting out of spite, go to Millie and tell her so. Clearly, you were frustrated and fed up with waiting for her, and you (correctly) felt that she had treated you disrespectfully. Be calm and polite when you talk to her, but make sure you've told your side of the story. Millie may end up apologizing to you, and after that you can work together to avoid future scheduling difficulties.

Let it blow over. Millie may be pouting now, but if she was paying attention when your boss scolded her, she knows perfectly well that she was the guilty party in your exchange. If you're absolutely sure you are in the right, and especially if you think Millie is likely to play politics with anything you say to her, your best strategy may be to say nothing. After a few days, initiate a casual conversation and see what happens. If she still refuses to speak to you, you'll know you need to find an opportunity to talk with her about what happened. If, on the other hand, she has calmed down and recognizes that you had a legitimate complaint, you can start rebuilding good relations without conceding any political capital.

Don't backbite. If Millie is chronically late getting information to you, she's probably doing the same thing to other people in the office. It can be all too easy to get defensive and to look for allies among your colleagues who are equally fed up with Millie's constant lateness. Don't give in to that temptation. If you start gossiping about Millie with your co-workers, she'll find out about it and you'll soon have a genuine need to apologize to her. Keep the matter between the two of you. The rest of the office doesn't need to be involved.

Head off future conflicts. By now, you know perfectly well that Millie is chronically late. Redesign your process for developing the report and, with your boss's approval, start asking Millie for the necessary information a few days earlier. She'll probably still be late, but the extra time will give you some latitude in getting the report done. You may also want to avoid scheduling social engagements on the evenings before your quarterly reports are due. That may mean missing the occasional opportunity to spend time with a friend, but it will reduce your stress level and increase your job satisfaction.

You Don't Know What You Did

Sometimes, you can find yourself in a situation in which someone seems to be angry with you, but you honestly don't know why, so you don't know what you ought to apologize for. Here's one example of such a situation:

Marie had some baby furniture that her toddler had outgrown. She loaned the furniture to her cousin Emily and her husband, Fred, who were expecting their first child. A few years went by, and Fred and Emily had four more children. They continued to use Marie's furniture and never offered to return it. Marie, who still hoped to have another child herself at some point, casually mentioned to Fred's mother, Pearl, that she'd like to get the baby furniture back from Fred and Emily once they were finished with it.

A few days later, Marie came home to find the baby furniture sitting on the front steps. When Marie tried to thank Fred and Emily for returning it, Emily abruptly changed the subject. Emily was cold with Marie from then on. Their relationship never fully recovered, and Marie never knew what she had done that so infuriated Emily.

If someone is angry with you, and you don't know why, you have several options for dealing with the situation.

Ask the other person. If you don't know why someone seems to be angry with you, it's not only okay to ask him or her, it's essential. Don't be concerned that the other person might be doubly offended that you don't even know what you did wrong. Unless you find out, you can't make amends, and it's entirely possible that the other person doesn't understand that you have a completely different point of view of the situation. Don't get defensive—just ask a simple question, and make it clear that you really want to know the answer.

Ask others. If you're too nervous to approach the other person directly, or if he or she won't talk to you at all, your next best option may be to try to find out from someone who knows you both why the other person is angry with you. (In Marie's case, asking Fred or Pearl might have given her the information she needed in order to make things right with Emily.) Be careful, though; if you don't ask the third party carefully, the person you've offended may think you're trying to round up allies behind his or her back.

Apologize anyway. One of the six essential elements of an effective apology is taking responsibility for your mistake, but that can be difficult to do if you don't know what mistake you made. Nothing says that your apology has to come in a specific order, however. If you honestly don't know what you did wrong and don't know how to find out, tell the person you have offended exactly that. You can then apologize and hope the other person will shed some light on your offense.

Stay calm. When you're apologizing for having done something without knowing what it is, your uncertainty can quickly turn to defensiveness and self-justification. You may find yourself becoming irritated with the other person, thinking that he or she should come out and tell you what you did wrong, but keep your annoyance under wraps. The goal is to heal the relationship, not to defend yourself. If your apology is effective, you can explain your side of the story later.

You're Both Too Upset to Talk about It

All too often, one person's mistake generates an angry response from the other, an argument ensues, and both parties walk away angry, hurt, and mutually deserving of an apology. When that happens to you, it can be tough to apologize first.

Let's say, for example, that your old friend Pat borrowed five hundred dollars from you to make a down payment on a new rental apartment. Six months later, when you ask Pat when he might be able to repay the loan, you discover that the down payment was only three hundred dollars, but Pat never bothered to tell you that or return the two hundred dollars he didn't need. Pat doesn't see it as a big deal—he thought you'd ask for the money when you wanted it, and feels as though you're being unreasonable. You, on the other hand, feel that your old friend has taken advantage of your generosity and essentially lied to you. You both lose your temper, the argument escalates out of control, and suddenly your longtime friendship seems to be over.

It's very human to want to hurt someone when he or she has hurt you. It can be very difficult to know when and how to respond when someone injures us, and most of us handle it badly at least some of the time. If you want to stay on good terms with the people around you, though, you'll have to accept that they, too, are human, and give them an opportunity to make amends when they make mistakes. In a situation in which you're too angry to talk, you have several options.

Weigh your feelings against the facts. Think about why you're so angry. Is this the first time Pat has borrowed money and not returned it, or has he done this numerous times over the years? Was there another situation in the past in which someone else borrowed money from you and failed to return it? How much of your anger with Pat goes back to your unresolved anger about that past experience? What is your family history with money? How hard was it for you to get the money together to give to him? For some people a five-hundred-dollar loan is a big deal, for others, not so much. Are you angry because of the amount of money involved, because Pat didn't bother to return the balance immediately, or because he got angry when you did? Are there other outstanding issues between the two of you?

Do you have your facts straight? Are you sure Pat understood that you expected him to return any unused balance on the loan as soon as he made the down payment? What do you think Pat should have done differently? Is this the first big argument you've had, or is this the final straw for you? Ultimately, what's more important to you—your friendship with Pat, or the anger you feel?

Your answers to these questions may surprise you. If your anger is based on a lot of long-standing resentment because Pat has abused your friendship in the past, you may decide that you simply aren't interested in being friends with Pat anymore. If you come to that conclusion, you may still want to forgive him, but you have the right to end a relationship, even a long-standing one, if you think it's in your best interest to do so. (We talked about these issues in Chapter 12, "How to Accept an Apology.")

If, on the other hand, you discover that your anger has less to do with Pat and more to do with your own circumstances—your family's attitude toward money, your own financial history, a bad experience with a loan to someone else, a general sense that people take advantage of you—you may be better able to put your anger at him in perspective. That will make it easier to apologize to Pat if you decide to do so.

Get a second opinion. If you're not sure whether you're overreacting, ask someone else whose judgment you trust—your spouse, a mutual friend, or your spiritual counselor. Tell the person you've consulted the whole story without whitewashing your own behavior, and make sure your advisor isn't just telling you what he or she thinks you want to hear. Too often, people ask for advice when all they really want is affirmation, so the people who love you may think they should tell you that you did the right thing, even if they don't really think so. Tell your advisor that you're really looking for his or her unvarnished opinion and not for a convenient way to excuse yourself. Then *listen*. You don't have to take your advisor's advice at face value or act on it in any particular way, but there's no sense in getting a second opinion if you aren't going to pay attention to it.

Be careful not to overdo it when seeking out advice. If you ask the opinions of half the people you and Pat both know, you may think you're getting input, but it will look to Pat as though you're trying to poison his relationships with your mutual friends. Your goal is to get a second opinion, not to line up a gang behind you. If one or two people tell you the same thing, that should give you enough feedback to decide how to proceed.

Let it settle. If your argument with Pat really got out of hand, it may be a while before he is ready to talk to you about it. Don't go charging in until you've both had reasonable time to cool off. However, if Pat hasn't contacted you after several days or weeks, and you still want to salvage the relationship, you'll probably have to get the ball rolling yourself. Don't wait too long—Pat may become doubly angry thinking you owe him an apology but couldn't be bothered to make it. Just let a little time go by, and then make the attempt.

Go first. In a situation in which both sides have caused offense, someone has to bite the bullet and apologize first. If you've decided that you want to stay friends with Pat, be mature about it and apologize. Going first doesn't make you a hero, so don't use it as proof that you're a bigger person than Pat. That will simply start a whole new argument. Just make the first overture, and let things progress from there.

The Other Person Won't Talk to You

If you find yourself in a situation in which you need to apologize, but the other person refuses to see you or talk to you, you still have options. For example, suppose your nasty Aunt Sadie made one too many snide remarks about your husband, and you loudly told her off in the middle of a family gathering. Aunt Sadie stormed out in a huff and hasn't spoken to you since. She won't take your calls or see you, but she's been making the rest of the family miserable with her complaints about your appalling behavior. Everyone agrees that Aunt Sadie is a witch, but they also think you overreacted to her sniping and they're tired of being in the middle. Even your husband agrees. What can you do?

Send a note. While written apologies are usually less effective than spoken ones delivered face-to-face, they may be your only option if the person you've offended won't give you a chance to apologize in person. Get out your good stationery (no typewritten letters or emails in this situation, please) and write the sincerest apology letter you can. Before you mail it, ask one or two other people in your family to read it and make sure you haven't accidentally said anything you shouldn't have. You want your apology to be effective, and if Aunt Sadie already isn't speaking to you, she'll probably be looking for reasons to criticize whatever you write.

Consider a gift. While apology gifts are often chancy in the business world, flowers might be a good peace offering when dealing with Aunt Sadie. Again, think before you order them. If she is allergic to roses, a dozen long-stemmed red ones won't help your cause. If you're able to order from a local shop, have the florist deliver your apology letter with the flowers. That way Aunt Sadie won't be able to claim she never got it, and she may be more likely to open it and read what you have to say if it comes with flowers attached.

Get some backup. Even if Aunt Sadie isn't speaking to you, she's probably still on good terms with someone else in your family who would be willing to intercede on your behalf. Don't go to every relative who was at the party looking for sympathy and support; just see if you can find one other person willing to plead your case with her. Don't ask that person to apologize to Aunt Sadie for you. Just ask him to tell Aunt Sadie how sorry you are about what happened and how much you regret what you did, and to ask her, please, to agree to talk with you. If your liaison is successful, you'll be able to apologize to Aunt Sadie in person and keep peace in your family.

Try, try again. Just because Aunt Sadie won't talk to you at first doesn't mean she won't talk to you at last. Keep trying, not necessarily every day, but frequently enough that she knows you're making a sincere effort to straighten things out with her. Eventually, her stubborn refusal to talk with you may begin to seem a little silly, even to her. If it does, you'll have your opportunity to apologize and make amends. If not, well, read on.

Let it go. After you've tried every alternative you can think of, and Aunt Sadie still won't talk to you months after you lost your temper with her, the problem is hers, not yours. If she's really determined never to speak to you again, there comes a point at which further attempts on your part to make peace aren't helpful, they're harassment.

Again, see what some of the other people in your family think before you call it quits. They're going to have to live with the consequences of a permanent rift between you and Aunt Sadie, too, so you should give them an opportunity to tell you if they think you're giving up too soon. Once you have a consensus that you've done all you can, though, send Aunt Sadie a final note wishing her well, and let it go.

No matter what you said to your Aunt Sadie, it probably wasn't bad enough to justify cutting you off completely. As futile as it may be to ask for forgiveness from Aunt Sadie, you may find that it's even harder to forgive yourself. If that's true, it might be a good idea to read Chapter 17 ("Forgiving Yourself").

CHAPTER 15

The Thirteen Most Common
Ways to Botch an Apology

*No doubt Jack the Ripper excused himself on
the grounds that it was human nature.*

—A. A. MILNE

As we have seen, developing and delivering an effective apology isn't
as easy as it may initially seem. However, most of the mistakes that
people make when apologizing fall into a very few categories. Avoid
these pitfalls, and your apology is much more likely to succeed.

Making Excuses

Of all the mistakes you can make when apologizing, making excuses is
the one that seems to annoy people the most. It's fine to explain why
you acted the way you did, and to describe any mitigating circumstances that might help the other person understand. The trick is to
describe what happened from your perspective without slipping over
the line into trying to justify your bad behavior or make yourself look
better. You already know that you need to apologize—there's no point
in trying to pretend that whatever you did really wasn't "all that bad."

Pointing Fingers

A common variation on making excuses is to try to shift the blame for
your mistake onto someone else. Don't do it. If you find yourself

about to say something like, "I never would have thrown that glass if John hadn't said. . . ," stop, take a deep breath, and shift direction. An effective apology requires you to take responsibility for your own actions, and you won't make yourself look any better by tarnishing someone else.

Above all, do not blame the person to whom you're apologizing for your bad behavior. If you shouldn't have shouted at the other person, for example, don't try to excuse yourself by saying he brought it on himself. An effective apology is about admitting to your own mistakes and saying you're sorry, not about shifting blame. Nothing you can say about someone else could possibly make you look, or be, better than an honest and straightforward apology will.

Clowning Around

Laughter may the best medicine, but joking when you make an apology is usually a very bad idea. Sincerity is essential to an effective apology, and laughter can kill sincerity. As tempting as it may be to try to lighten the mood with a joke while you're apologizing, resist the urge. People are often nervous and uncomfortable when apologizing, and making a joke can seem like a great way to break the tension. However, unless you're extremely careful about what you say, and the other person recognizes that the joke isn't pointed at her, you're likely to make matters a lot worse, especially if the other person decides that you're laughing *at* her.

Even jokes at your own expense can be risky. You may be clearly laughing at yourself, but it may seem to the other person that what you're really trying to do is minimize what you did wrong so you won't have to make a genuine apology or suffer any real remorse. The primary purpose of an apology is to mend fences with the injured person, not to make you feel better. If you top an apology off with a joke, you risk sounding careless, phony, and self-serving. An apology is not a joking matter.

To that end, never suggest that the other person ought to lighten up and appreciate your joking. Telling someone you've offended that he or she lacks a sense of humor is a great way to add insult to injury. Hold off on the wisecracks until the other person has accepted your apology and some time has passed. There will be plenty of opportunities to share a laugh then.

Denying Wrongdoing

If you've ever received an apology from someone that started with "I'm sorry you're mad at me," you know how ineffective such an "apology" can be. Referencing the other person's anger or hurt without admitting you did something offensive is just another way of shrugging off responsibility. What you're essentially saying is that you're not sorry for what you did, but you're not happy that the other person is angry or upset. That's not an apology, it's a cop-out, and it may further enrage the person you have already offended.

If you truly believe you did nothing wrong and you can't bring yourself to admit that you could have handled a situation better, your best option may be to say something like, "I know you're angry, and I feel very badly about that. What can I do to make things better between us?" A statement along those lines may open up the lines of communication with the other person enough to eventually lead to better relations. But it isn't exactly an apology.

Playing a Scene

Some people apologize with a lot of drama—tears, hand-wringing, high-pitched avowals of everlasting remorse, and so forth. That kind of melodramatic behavior is almost never appropriate in a business or public setting, and usually falls flat even in the most intimate personal settings. Unless you're very sure that the person you have offended will understand and appreciate a high-intensity apology, go for a sincere, restrained approach. Empty theatrics will only make you look insincere, and nothing destroys an apology more effectively than insincerity.

Using the "i" Word

How often have you heard a public figure, whether an elected official or a Hollywood celebrity, start an apology by saying, "I'm sorry *if* my actions injured or offended anyone"? Here's a classic from the late Richard M. Nixon, taken from his speech to the nation when he resigned from the U.S. presidency in the wake of the Watergate scandal, on August 8, 1974:

> I regret deeply any injuries that may have been done in the course of events that have led to this decision. I would say only that *if* some of my judgments were wrong, and they were wrong, they were made in what I believed at the time to be in the best interest of the nation. (emphasis added)

The use of that two-letter word, *if,* is enough to make what might have been an effective apology completely meaningless. When you've gotten to the point of making an apology, you already know that your actions injured or offended someone. If you didn't, you wouldn't be apologizing for what you did. Skip the *if,* and get to the point.

Demanding Forgiveness

Some people believe that once they say the words "I'm sorry," all should be immediately forgiven. Nothing could be further off base. As we have already seen, some misdeeds are almost impossible to forgive, and many more will be forgiven only after enough time has passed for mutual trust between the wrongdoer and the injured person to be restored. Even when an apology has been accepted, relations may never be the same. Depending on the circumstances, the person you have injured may forgive you, but that doesn't mean he or she is required to forget what happened or pretend nothing has changed. Apologize because you think you should, not because you think it will instantly erase the consequences. And be prepared to wait awhile before you're forgiven.

Timing It Wrong

A quick apology delivered off the cuff rarely sounds sincere. If you've ever watched a courtroom drama on television, you've seen this scenario: One of the attorneys asks a witness an improper question. The other attorney objects and the first attorney, perhaps even before the judge can say a word, tosses off quickly, "I'll withdraw it." All the procedural rules of the courtroom have been observed, but the question hangs in the air, lingering in the minds of the television audience and, presumably, the jurors who will decide the case. An apology that comes too quickly and easily is a lot like that "I'll withdraw it"—it may satisfy the technical rules of social behavior, but it probably won't be enough to erase your mistake from the mind of the person you offended.

Conversely, if you wait too long to apologize for a mistake, your apology is just as likely to fall flat. For example, suppose you disagreed with a colleague in a meeting with your boss and, in an effort to promote your own approach to solving a problem, aggressively belittled your colleague's recommendations. If you waited weeks to apologize to your colleague for your behavior, anything you said would likely sound a lot less sincere than it would have if you'd apologized within a few hours of the meeting. You shouldn't apologize until you're ready to do so, but dragging your feet will make it very difficult for you to mend fences.

Apologizing Privately for a Public Offense

If you've said or done something that embarrassed or offended someone else in a public setting, apologizing in private probably won't do
the job. For example, if you made a nasty crack about a colleague's
"incompetence" at a meeting with a client, apologizing to your colleague after the client has left won't undo the damage. Make sure that
anyone who witnessed your behavior either witnesses or is made
aware of the apology, so your colleague isn't left wondering whether
his relationship with the client has been damaged or not.

Picking the Wrong Medium

If you could easily have apologized in person but chose another
medium instead, the other person is likely to recognize that you took
the coward's way out. For example, sending an email to apologize to a
co-worker whose office is ten feet away from yours is a great way to
ensure that your apology will fail. If you find you're extremely
tempted to avoid a face-to-face apology, that's probably because you
made a major mistake that only a face-to-face apology can remedy.
Use the medium that is most likely to seem sincere.

Dropping the Ball

If you've promised to do something in particular to make amends for
your mistake, your apology will fall short if you don't follow through.
If, for example, you promised to give a disappointed customer a special discount on all future purchases, don't cut it off after a single
transaction or, even worse, fail to tell your sales team that the customer is green-lighted for special treatment. If anything, deliver more
than you promised. Don't hold back on someone you've disappointed.

Repeating Your Offense

Bad habits can be hard to break, and promises to behave better in the future can be difficult to keep. If, for example, you have a chronic tendency to take on too many projects at one time, the client you disappoint with a late product may forgive you once, twice, or even three times. Eventually, though, you'll lose that client's confidence and maybe even lose the client to a competitor who's more reliable. Cut your schedule back to something more reasonable, and make sure your client knows the delays won't happen again.

Never Apologizing at All

Any apology, no matter how badly phrased or poorly delivered, is likely to be more effective than none at all. If you've done something to offend someone else, the worst thing you can do is to ignore the matter and hope it goes away. We've already seen that there are many good reasons to apologize, and many effective ways to do so. Pick your best option, and go to it.

PART FOUR

AFTER THE APOLOGY

CHAPTER 16

After You Apologize

I can give you a six-word formula for success: "Think things through—then follow through."

—Sir Walter Scott

Once you've delivered your apology and the injured party has had an opportunity to respond, you may be satisfied that everything has been worked out between you. Depending on the circumstances, however, you may also find that you still have more work to do to make things right. There are some things that frequently need to be addressed after you've made your initial apology.

Follow Through

One of the essential elements of an effective apology is making amends for whatever you did to offend the other person. While you may be able to do that right away in some situations, in others it may take you some time to wrap everything up, and still others may require a long-term commitment. To use a workplace example, if you were late with a project for an important client, making amends with your boss might include calling the client to apologize personally for the delay and fully answering all of the client's follow-up questions. Your apology to your boss won't be effective unless and until you've talked to the client and satisfied her concerns.

Following through can be more difficult if you're apologizing for the latest manifestation of one of your chronic shortcomings. For example, suppose you made the mistake of telling your fair-haired administrative assistant a "blonde joke"—you thought it was funny, but she clearly disagreed. If it's the first time you've made that particular gaffe, your follow-through will be relatively simple: Don't tell her any more blonde jokes, and be a little more sensitive to her dignity thereafter. On the other hand, if this is the fourth or fifth time you've offended her with a similar joke, you'll have to be much more careful and self-disciplined about inflicting your sense of humor on her in the future. Don't brush this off as a minor annoyance, by the way. If you tell your administrative assistant enough offensive jokes, you'll create the kind of hostile environment that leads to lawsuits. Here is a simple rule of thumb: Every mistake sets you back some distance with the person you have offended. The more setbacks you have, the longer it will take for you to follow through, bridge the distance, and put the relationship back together.

Thoughtless behavior won't do you any good at work, but it can be even more hurtful to a spouse, child, or personal friend. Injured feelings can lastingly damage the trust in a personal relationship, so it's especially important to follow through when making amends to a loved one. Let's say, for example, that you agreed to take your son to a movie on a particular Saturday afternoon, but got caught up in cleaning out the garage, lost track of time, and ended up missing the screening. One way to make amends might be to promise to take him to the movie the next day, but you'd better be prepared to follow through on that promise. Your son will be watching carefully to make sure you're as good as your word. If you break your promise again, you'll teach him that you really can't be trusted and, perhaps, that he doesn't need to keep his promises to you, either.

Stick with It

If you've severely injured someone else, a single apology may not be enough to make matters right between you. If, for example, you made a serious mistake in a memorandum you sent to your boss, it may be a while before your boss trusts you to produce error-free work. Be extra careful about checking your work for a while, and recognize that it may take time to regain your boss's trust. This is related to the follow-through discussed above. If you don't stick with your follow-through, you'll just repeat the same mistake and find yourself apologizing all over again.

The same is true at home, of course. If you bounce a check from a joint bank account, it's entirely understandable for your spouse to be a little nervous about trusting you with the family finances again. Even if it feels as if you're being unfairly scrutinized, take a deep breath and be more careful about the money you spend until your spouse decides it's safe to relax.

Circle Back

Once you've made your initial apology and a little time has passed, consider whether you need to touch base with the other person again to make sure things are all right between you. This may be almost impossible if the other person is a stranger, but even then, it never hurts to add an extra "are you okay?" before leaving an encounter with a stranger to whom you've had to apologize.

If, on the other hand, the offended person is someone you know at least a little, and an opportunity presents itself, checking in one more time can be a great way to ensure that your initial apology has been accepted. Here's an example of just such an incident:

Jeanne was at a party the first night of her beach vacation, when she met Marty, a conference-center manager, and his wife, Sarah. They got to talking over cocktails, and Marty made it very clear that he was interested in having his center host one of Jeanne's company conferences. When Marty asked Jeanne to go for a walk with him after dinner, Jeanne assumed it was to discuss how Marty could submit a bid proposal for her company's upcoming conference. Marty, however, had enjoyed several glasses of wine with dinner and had a different proposal in mind. He grabbed Jeanne and kissed her. Jeanne, shocked, pushed him away, but not before Sarah witnessed the whole thing. Sarah shrieked, a scene ensued, and Jeanne left the party feeling humiliated and unhappy.

The next day, Jeanne was unsure of what to do. She didn't think she had done anything wrong, but she knew how upset Sarah had been and was concerned that Sarah might believe she had done something to lead Marty on. Jeanne also knew that she'd probably be seeing the couple throughout the week, and she didn't want Sarah to think she didn't care about her feelings. Jeanne went to talk to them. Luckily, by then Marty had confessed to Sarah that he had initiated the kiss without any encouragement, and Sarah knew Jeanne hadn't been responsible for what happened. Marty apologized to Jeanne, Jeanne apologized to Sarah for having upset her, and Sarah acknowledged, somewhat grudgingly, that Jeanne wasn't to blame.

Jeanne left, but was still a little uncomfortable with how the apology had gone. She asked her friend Jeff, who knew Sarah far better than she did, to talk to her privately and reassure her that Jeanne had not encouraged Marty and was just as upset about the whole situation as Sarah was. A few days later, after Jeff and Sarah had spoken, Jeanne found an opportunity to talk to Sarah again. She asked Sarah whether things were all right between them, and Sarah assured her that they were. That second conversation gave Sarah an opportunity for further conversation if she needed it, and let both women come to closure on the embarrassing incident.

As with so many other aspects of an effective apology, circling back can be especially important when you've had to apologize to someone you love. Personal relationships can be fraught with complex and sometimes conflicting emotions, and an apology that seems adequate at first may not seem so after some time has passed. Let's say, for example, that you got into an argument with your mother-in-law, and you both said some ugly things. The next day, you went to see her and apologized. The conversation went well, apologies were exchanged and accepted, and you left thinking that everything was fine. Unfortunately, your mother-in-law continued to brood about what you had said during a bout of insomnia that night and by the next day she was upset all over again. Circling back a day or two later could give you an opportunity to make things right again, instead of letting lingering bad feelings sour your relationship with her.

Some people are reluctant to circle back and bring the matter up again. It can be a matter of embarrassment or just sheer weariness of addressing an emotionally taxing topic. Consequently, it's often tempting to say, "But I already made my apology. If I bring the whole mess up again, won't that be overdoing it? When do I get to be done?"

The answer, of course, depends on the situation. If your initial apology went well and you're absolutely confident that you resolved matters with the person you injured, you may choose not to circle back. If you still have lingering doubts, though, or if the other person seems unusually cool afterward, find an opportunity to make sure things are right between the two of you. Circling back demonstrates your sincerity far better than maintaining a strained silence does.

Prevent a Replay

It's always important, after making an apology, to do better next time. One way to do that can be to put safeguards in place to preempt your repeating the same mistake. Sometimes just a simple shift in how you do things can make a tremendous preventive difference. For example, a hospital got in legal trouble when a nurse failed to dilute a medication with the proper amount of saline solution prior to injecting a patient, and the patient suffered serious injuries as a result of the accidental overdose. As part of its apology to the patient and her family, the hospital agreed to implement new safeguards to prevent other patients from suffering the same misfortune. By taping bottles of saline to the medication on the storage shelf, the hospital made it easier for busy nurses to remember not to administer the medication undiluted.

Should You Ask to Be Forgiven?

Some people believe that asking for forgiveness is an essential element of an effective apology, but forgiveness doesn't always immediately follow. The other person may not be ready or able to forgive you when you first apologize, particularly if you've done something that really hurt or offended him or her. If that's the case, asking for forgiveness may put unfair pressure on the offended person to grant you forgiveness before he or she is ready or able to do so. That isn't an effective way to apologize. Here's an example of a situation in which a request for forgiveness came too soon:

Barbara and Morgan were in a staff meeting with their company's general counsel and the chief executive officer discussing a disappointed customer's threat to sue. At one point, the attorney and the CEO got into a private conversation. Barbara leaned over and hissed to Morgan, "If you hadn't mishandled that customer in the first place, we wouldn't be in this mess. Now look where we are, and it's all your fault!" Morgan was stunned and angry, but didn't want to argue with Barbara in a public meeting, especially when she wasn't sure the other people present had heard Barbara's whispered accusation. She sat through the rest of the meeting in silence, steaming.

After the meeting, Barbara invited Morgan to lunch, and seemed genuinely surprised when Morgan refused to go. When Morgan pointed out that Barbara had blamed her for the pending lawsuit and embarrassed her in front of the attorney and the CEO, Barbara replied, offhandedly, "Did I? I apologize. Can you forgive me?"

Whatever Barbara's intentions may have been, her glib apology and immediate request for forgiveness offended Morgan all over again. If Barbara had waited to give Morgan time to calm down and then offered her a sincere apology, Morgan might have been willing to forgive her. As it was, their relationship never fully recovered.

The fact that you owe someone an apology does not mean they owe you forgiveness the instant you say you're sorry—or ever. Ask forgiveness only when you truly think it's deserved and when you can do so without twisting the other person's arm. Otherwise, leave it to the other person to give you the gift of forgiveness when he or she is ready to do so.

*   *   *   *

The steps you take after making your apology can be just as important as the apology itself. Ultimately, your sincerity will be judged not only by your words but also by your actions. Following the steps in this chapter can significantly increase the likelihood that your apology will lead to lasting reconciliation.

CHAPTER 17

Forgiving Yourself

*The depth of your compassion lies in
your ability to forgive yourself.*

—MARK GRAHAM

An important, and often unaddressed, aspect of having to make an apology is coming to terms within yourself with what you did wrong. Even after you've apologized to people you've injured, and your apology has been accepted, you may find it difficult to forgive yourself. If you're embarrassed by something you've done, if you destroyed a once-in-a-lifetime opportunity through a careless or foolish mistake, or if you have injured someone you cared about and weren't able or willing to apologize, or to do it effectively or in time, you're likely to have lasting regrets and lingering shame.

I'm not a professional psychologist, but I know from personal experience that it's not a good idea to try simply to forget your mistakes and bad actions. No matter how hard you push them away, memories of times when you acted badly are likely to linger in the back of your mind until you can forgive yourself. Unresolved guilt and embarrassment can haunt you for years, undermining your self-confidence and thwarting you as you attempt to do better in the future.

If you find yourself struggling with a lot of unresolved issues, the advice of a professional therapist may help you improve your inner balance. However, if you want to minimize the impact on your self-esteem of more recent mistakes, consider apologizing to yourself as you would to anyone else you hurt or offended.

Write Yourself a Letter

You can apologize to yourself out loud, and although this can be effective, it can deny you the chance to explore your feelings fully. Writing yourself a letter of apology can be a more effective way of moving toward self-forgiveness, because it allows you to dig deeply into your feelings about why you did what you did and the ensuing consequences. Plus, you'll be able to keep the letter and read it as many times as necessary.

Write the letter in your diary or journal, or in any other medium. Keep it in a private place—it's usually not a good idea to keep a record of an apology to yourself anywhere that someone else might read it— and read it as often as you need to until you're able to forgive yourself.

The six elements of an effective apology are a little different when you apologize to yourself, but they're as important in this situation as in any other. To use an illustrative example, let's say that your boss, seemingly arbitrarily, denied your request for leave over Christmas, which meant that you had to disappoint your family. When he was out of his office a few days later, you snuck in and broke his treasured golf trophy to get even. (Don't laugh—a case much like this really happened.) You knew it was childish and stupid when you did it, and you regretted your actions the instant the trophy broke, but there was no way to repair the trophy without being found out. Your boss doesn't know who did the damage, and now you're feeling very guilty and frightened of what he might do if he ever figured it out. Here's how the six essential elements of an effective apology to yourself might apply.

Take reasonable responsibility. In your apology to yourself, describe what you did wrong, but don't overstate it. (It's also possible you'll unfairly downplay what you did, but if you're ashamed enough to be giving yourself an apology, you're more likely to inflate than to minimize.) Yes, you deliberately broke your boss's golf trophy, but it probably won't help if you describe what you did as a "vile, malicious act of vicious and senseless vandalism." You acted badly and you're right to be ashamed, but it's not as though you took a chainsaw to the *Mona Lisa*. (And don't forget your boss's contribution—if he'd been reasonable about your leave request or even apologetic, you might not have reacted so badly.) Keeping what you did in perspective will help you to forgive yourself, so you can better decide what you need to do next.

Explore your feelings. Write a few sentences about how you felt when you were acting out, and how you feel about it now. Were you angry, disappointed, frustrated, or some combination of all three? Did you feel as though your boss had been nasty, controlling, or unfair in denying your leave request? How do you feel about things now? Would you go back in time and handle things differently if you could? It's important to recognize the extent to which any bad feelings have been transformed over time into genuine remorse, which will help you to forgive yourself. By the same token, if you find that you're still angry and not really sorry you broke the trophy, your feelings may not be admirable, but at least they're honest. Your next step may be to stop apologizing to yourself for damaging the trophy and to start looking for a new job. Exploring your feelings will also help you find out where the limits of your self-control are, which may help you avoid taking similar actions in the future.

Put your shortcomings into perspective. The simple fact that you're ashamed by what you did indicates that you're not a person who routinely acts maliciously. Are you someone who goes around every day looking for opportunities to damage other people's prized possessions? Probably not: In all likelihood, you're usually polite, respectful, and careful of other people and their things, just as most of us are. The fact that you had a bad moment doesn't make you a bad person, nor does a single mistake mean that you need to beat yourself up endlessly.

If, on the other hand, you realize that you often react to disappointment by secretly injuring other people, you need to learn better ways to deal with your anger and frustration, perhaps with the help of a professional counselor. Chapter 18, "Learning from Your Apologies," can help you decide if what you did was an isolated incident or part of a larger pattern.

Acknowledge your better side in your letter, and recognize that your bad moment was an exception to your rule of good behavior. If you honestly can't think of anything good to say about yourself to balance out the bad, you have bigger issues than this one incident. Seek out some professional counseling so you can get a more balanced perspective on your actions and emotions.

Commit to mending fences. Think about what you can do to make amends. This may not be easy to do. You certainly could confess to your boss and pay to have the trophy repaired or replaced. That would be an honorable way to handle the incident. However, doing that could cost you your job, so confessing might not be a practical solution, even though it would be the most ethical one. Think through alternatives, and come up with something you can manage (even if it's a little painful). For example, perhaps you can simply tell your boss how sorry you are that the trophy was damaged and help him find the best place to have it repaired. Just the act of searching for a way to make things right will help you feel better about yourself and make your apology to yourself more effective.

Accept your humanity. As nice as it would be never to make a mistake or act badly, you're a human being, so you're not perfect. Neither, by the way, is anyone else. While regret and remorse within reason are the right response to your bad behavior, too much self-abuse is nothing more than pride gone wrong. Don't make the mistake of assuming that no one else would ever have done what you did, or that you're somehow uniquely flawed because you had a bad moment. You showed bad judgment—that doesn't make you a monster.

Do better hereafter. By now, you should have a pretty good idea of what was motivating you when you broke the trophy, so you can use that knowledge to figure out how to avoid making a similar misstep in the future. Promise yourself, in writing, that you'll do better in the future, and be as specific as possible about what you'll do to make that happen. Maybe it's taking a walk around the block when you're tempted to damage something, putting your frustrations on paper and then burning it, or finding a job where you have more control over your schedule. Whatever it is, promise yourself that you'll do better next time, and keep that promise to the best of your ability thereafter.

* * * *

Forgiving yourself for your own mistakes is essential to being able to forgive others, and also to living comfortably with yourself. It can be easier to forgive yourself if you're able to learn from your apologies (and the transgressions that made them necessary). We'll address that in the next chapter.

CHAPTER 18

Learning from Your Apologies

Mistakes are the portals of discovery.

—James Joyce

Some people think of an apology as a gift you give to someone else to make up for having hurt or offended that person. Others think of an apology as the price you pay to obtain the other person's forgiveness. Neither is quite right.

In most cases, a gift is something you can choose to give or not. (Even in a situation in which a gift seems mandatory—your spouse's birthday, perhaps—you made the choice to get married, so you voluntarily took on the responsibility to provide birthday gifts as part of your marital relationship.) An apology, by contrast, is something you owe to the other person. You really can't expect to stay on good terms with that person if you don't pay the debt.

On the other hand, even though you may owe that person an apology, he or she is not automatically obliged to forgive you simply because you apologized. The forgiveness, not the apology, is the gift. It's lovely to receive (and will usually come if you've apologized sincerely), but it's not something to which you're entitled. Remember, you created your obligation to apologize by offending the other person, and your apology simply "balances the scale." It doesn't guarantee you'll get anything more.

Luckily, every apology comes with its own gift to you: the opportunity to learn from it. Any mistake can teach you something, but apologies offer a special opportunity to learn because they teach you where your weaknesses are and how you can interact better with other people. Interpersonal skills are essential to success in practically every aspect of life, so learning from your apologies can help you succeed in every setting.

Look for Patterns

Are there certain apologies you find yourself making again and again? Are you chronically late for meetings, consistently behind schedule in finishing assignments, or always apologizing for errors in your work? Do you find yourself apologizing frequently for making unkind jokes, losing your temper, forgetting appointments, or hurting other people's feelings? If so, don't torture yourself—just recognize that you have some all-too-human weaknesses, and that you need to do something to correct or compensate for them.

Another pattern to look for is whether you find yourself apologizing repeatedly to the same people. Are you always apologizing to your boss, your administrative assistant, your spouse, your best friend, your mother-in-law? That might indicate a problem that stems from the other person, not you. If, after careful consideration, you decide that the other person is really the problem—your boss is ridiculously demanding, your spouse is hypersensitive, your mother-in-law is always looking for a fight—it will probably change your attitude. You may still end up apologizing to that person again and again because you decide that, in the larger scheme of things, it's worth paying that price. Then again, you may decide that it's time to start standing up for yourself and refusing to apologize when you've done nothing wrong. Either way, you can rest easier in your own mind knowing the other person is the problem, and you are not.

If, on the other hand, you notice that you're constantly apologizing to a particular person who's done nothing to provoke your bad behavior, it's time to look at the relationship. What is it about that person that tempts you to act badly toward him or her? Are you jealous? Do you take his or her goodwill for granted? Do you resent that person's claim on your time? Figure out what's causing you to act badly toward that person, and straighten things out.

When it comes to dealing with loved ones, patterns often abound because relationships fall into habits. If there's something about a friend, family member, or your spouse that frequently moves you to bad behavior, see if you can't change your attitude. Let's say, for example, that your husband routinely promises to wash the dirty dishes after dinner and, just as routinely, leaves them in the sink until the next day or two. If you find yourself repeatedly apologizing to him for losing your temper over the unwashed dishes, you can probably deduce that it's more important to you than it is to him to wake up to a clean kitchen. At that point, ask yourself what matters more to you—clean dishes or a happy marriage? If your marriage wins out, find a way to solve the problem before you blow up again. Maybe you can wash the dishes together, or you can simply wash them yourself because it's more important to you than it is to him to get them cleaned up before you go to bed.

If you notice that you frequently owe apologies to a whole group of people, it's time to take a harder look at yourself. Are you always apologizing to the women or the men in your life? You may be more sexist than you realize. Do you find you often have to apologize to older people? Perhaps you have less respect for their age and wisdom than you should. Do you apologize more than once a month or so to your children? If so, maybe you should reconsider the superior attitude that leads you to be impatient or rude with them in the first place.

The point of looking for patterns in your apologies is not to shame yourself—it's to identify areas of your life where you're often unable to behave as well as you would like. Study your apologies now and then. If you observe a pattern, make an effort to address the underlying reasons for your misbehavior.

Look for Reasons

If the patterns in your apologies suggest that your intentions are good but you have a chronic shortcoming, what you need to do is come up with a way to compensate. No one is good at everything, so don't waste time wishing you were perfect—just focus on how to get better, because better will probably be good enough.

What is motivating you? First, figure out why you act in a way that makes you obliged to apologize so often. If, for example, you're always late with projects because you take on too much work, look at why you do that. Are you afraid that if you aren't constantly juggling too much work, people will think you're lazy or unproductive? Do you fear being replaced by someone younger or with different credentials? Are you reluctant to go home at night because there are troubles in your marriage? Do you fill your time with more work than you can handle because you have nothing better to do? Ask yourself some gentle questions, and see what emerges. You may find that your apologies over your inability to finish work on time have little to do with your job, and a lot to do with your personal life.

What can you do to improve? If you chronically take on too much work because you're trying to impress your boss, set a limit on how many projects you're willing to juggle at one time, and stick to it. The chances are good that your boss will be happier with the overall quality of your work if you do a better, more efficient job with the work you take on. If you think people around you see you as lazy and unproductive, ask them. Their answers may surprise you, and may let you rest more easily.

What works at the office probably works even better at home. If you're always apologizing to your family for dropping one ball or another, are you trying to do too much? Maybe the house doesn't have to be immaculate, dinner doesn't always have to be a gourmet affair, every stitch of clothing on your family's back doesn't have to be color coordinated and perfectly laundered, and you don't have to attend every soccer game your kids play. Yes, it's important to do nice things for your spouse and children, but taking on more than you can handle is a recipe for disappointment all around. Talk to your family and decide what can be simplified, so you won't have so much to juggle.

What problems have you been avoiding? If you realize that your apologies are linked to problems with your choices or attitudes, you may have a harder time making things right. Suppose, for example, you realize that you're constantly apologizing for mistakes you make at work because you really hate what you do for a living. It's probably time to think about how to improve the situation. Maybe you need to switch jobs, change professions, go back to school, retire, or go into business for yourself.

Similarly, if an honest examination of your apologies leads you to realize that you're constantly messing up at home because you're unhappy in your marriage or family situation, you probably have some hard work to do. What's making you so unhappy? What could you do to improve things? Is the problem something you can address by yourself, or do you need to talk about it with a loved one? Let's say, for example, that you're constantly apologizing to your teenage son for losing your temper during political discussions. One of you is liberal, the other conservative, and you don't seem able to spend ten minutes at the dinner table without blowing your stack over your son's opinions. Maybe you realize that you're the one who always starts the argument, so the answer is for you to find other things to talk about. Maybe your son picks the fights, in which case you need to have a calm conversation with him about finding better ways for the two of you to agree to disagree. Or maybe the political arguments are just a symptom of a deeper rift between you and your son that needs to be addressed with the help of a family counselor. Whatever is causing the problem, your apologies are pointing you in the right direction to fix it.

As another, perhaps more painful, example, if an honest look at yourself reveals that you secretly believe that other people should always defer to your wishes, and you find yourself regularly apologizing for getting unreasonably angry when they don't, ask yourself why you think you're entitled to that level of reverence. Maybe your expectations are unrealistic, or you're harboring outdated prejudices that other people don't accept. If you conclude that in the privacy of your own thoughts you're a bit of a racist, sexist, ageist, or what have you, it's probably past time that you changed your attitude. You may find the advice of a career counselor, a spiritual advisor, or a therapist helpful in coming to a better understanding of why you feel the way you do. You don't have to change your beliefs if you don't want to, but if you're constantly apologizing, it's probably wise for you to consider the possibility that your beliefs aren't serving you well.

Map Out a Strategy

Once you've figured out what motivates you to keep acting in a particular way for which you are compelled to apologize, begin to develop a plan to compensate for your weak spot. You may not be able to change your behavior overnight, or even at all, but you can certainly change the circumstances around you. If, for example, you're chronically overcommitted, try politely turning down every other assignment that comes your way. There are many polite ways to say no, so don't assume that you'll be fired the instant you suggest you have too much to do to take on any more. If overcommitment has been enough of a problem that you have had to apologize frequently for it, your co-workers and boss are well aware of the problem and will probably applaud your new resolve. If you're chronically late for meetings and appointments, try setting your watch five minutes early, or allowing ten extra minutes for traffic whenever you set out to meet someone. If you find you really begrudge the extra time, take something with you that you can do if you arrive early. If you're always apologizing to your kids for being too tired to play with them, set up a schedule for yourself that includes adequate rest and exercise. Be sure to stick with it, and build family playtime into your weekly routine.

Try, try again. If you have had to apologize more than once for a particular kind of mistake, the odds are good that you won't be able to correct or compensate for that mistake the first, or even the tenth, time you try. For example, if you've gotten into the habit of switching on the television every night and ignoring your spouse, it's likely going to take a concerted effort on your part to resist the urge to reach for the remote and instead invite your spouse to take a walk with you or just sit back and talk. Even then, you may be likely to fall back into the television habit whenever you're exhausted, under too much pressure, or tempted by a program that promises to be particularly engrossing. Experts say that it takes a minimum of three months to break a bad habit, so recognize that you didn't get into the habit of mindlessly watching television overnight, and you probably won't change it overnight, either. Don't beat yourself up if you backslide— just see where things went wrong and try again. Eventually, your persistence will pay off, and you'll find yourself apologizing less often for that particular mistake.

Once is enough. While the patterns in your apologies can teach you a lot about yourself, some apologies involve mistakes that are so significant that you shouldn't ever repeat them. If, for example, you're caught sexually harassing someone subordinate to you at work, and you're lucky enough to be allowed to keep your job after you apologize, don't make that apology the first in a series. Recognize the apology as a warning, and change your attitude and behavior before they get you in permanent trouble. The same is true if you're caught cheating on your spouse or gambling away the family's savings. Apologize at once and, if you're forgiven, get whatever help you need to avoid making the same mistake again. You may not get a second chance to do so.

*   *   *   *

The reasons for apologies are as individual as fingerprints. Study yours and, over time, they'll help you learn to deal better with people in every avenue of your life.

CHAPTER 19

Creating an Apology-Friendly Workplace

We make a living by what we get, but
we make a life by what we give.

—Winston Churchill

One of the best gifts you can give to yourself and your co-workers is an apology-friendly working environment. Even if you're not the boss, don't assume that your hands are tied. Management may have the most direct impact on company policies, but no matter where you fall in the office hierarchy, you can have a positive influence on the tone of your workplace. Practice the principles in this chapter at work, and encourage those who work with you to do the same. (If nothing else, you can always leave a copy of this book on your boss's desk.)

The Fundamentals of an Apology-Friendly Environment

Some people worry that the quality of their company's goods and services will suffer if employees find it easy to apologize for their errors. As we saw in "Apologies in the Workplace" (Chapter 6), however, even the best companies are run by fallible human beings, and failing to deal with mistakes when they happen can lead to disaster. This is not to say that your company should tolerate bad behavior or shoddy work. However, even the most careful, skilled, and dedicated employees make mistakes. If you encourage your colleagues to acknowledge and apologize for their mistakes, your company will ultimately prosper for it.

On the other hand, if your work environment is so harsh that employees are afraid to admit to their mistakes, your company will suffer in at least two respects. First, your best employees will be likely to leave when presented with opportunities to work in more forgiving environments, and they can readily do so because they have marketable skills. Companies with unforgiving work cultures can find it difficult to retain talent, and frequently suffer the loss of employees' specialized skills and institutional memory. An environment that drives away the best while keeping the worst is sure to become a breeding ground for mediocrity, and employee morale is likely to go from bad to worse over time.

Second, employees who choose (or are forced) to stay on in an unforgiving work environment may try to hide their mistakes from management for fear of being disciplined or losing their jobs. If they're successful at this, management is likely to learn about problems too late to solve them. For example, imagine that one of your employees made a significant cost projection error in a contract bid proposal, and discovered the mistake after the bid proposal was submitted but before the contract was awarded. If your company maintained an apology-friendly atmosphere so that your employee was not afraid to notify management of the error, you might have the opportunity to withdraw or modify the bid. If, on the other hand, your employee was too afraid to admit to the mistake in time to correct it, your company could end up winning the contract but having to perform it at a significant financial loss. Your failure to provide the employee with an environment in which he or she could safely acknowledge the error could be disastrously expensive.

Creating an apology-friendly environment takes time and effort, but it can enhance productivity and employee loyalty. As you work to create that environment, there are some factors to keep in mind.

Banish perfectionism. While work that is sloppy, incomplete, or seriously wrong isn't acceptable, there comes a point with almost any endeavor in which the perfect becomes the enemy of the good. Let's say, for example, that a project team in your company was responsible for developing a thousand-page technical report loaded with tables, graphs, charts, and mathematical formulas. If the team produces a marvelous report that meets the needs of the assignment and satisfies your client, think twice before criticizing the team members if you find a minor typographical error in one footnote. The message you'll send to your team is that the vast majority of their good work was diminished by a minuscule mistake, and they'll come away feeling disappointed with the project despite its overall high quality. They may be less enthusiastic about the next big project. They may even be less careful about catching errors if they believe that they'll be criticized no matter how good their work is.

Overcoming perfectionism can also help you protect your company from expensive litigation. Particularly in the context of professional malpractice litigation, the courts have generally held that professionals are required to comply with generally accepted practices and to use good professional judgment, but have not ruled that professionals are never allowed to make a mistake or must guarantee that nothing will ever go wrong. Thus, for example, a doctor who performs surgery on a patient is not normally responsible if the patient dies on the operating table, so long as the doctor followed accepted medical procedures and was appropriately careful in diagnosing and treating the patient's illness. However, nothing prevents a professional from setting a higher standard for himself or herself, and the courts will generally enforce a professional firm's policies to the extent that they become promises to clients. If you insist on perfection from your employees, a disappointed client may use that fact in court to demonstrate that perfection is your firm's policy and you promised more than you could reasonably deliver.

Setting more rational expectations in your office can help protect you from that risk.

Educate your customers. Make sure your customers know that while you're very good at what you do, mistakes will happen from time to time. Give good service, but don't promise more than you can reasonably deliver. Tell your customers if you think a transaction is likely to go wrong, apologize, and make reasonable amends if your actions created the problem. If your customers know not to expect the impossible, they'll be more likely to forgive you and work with you to solve problems when they arise. Let's say, for example, that you're a clothing manufacturer and you're going to be late shipping an order of blouses, because your supplier couldn't provide the quantity of fabric needed to complete the order, and you can't get any more for several days. If your customer already knows that your shipping dates aren't guarantees, but rather estimates based on the availability of needed supplies, she's less likely to be unhappy when you have to tell her that your blouses will ship later than expected.

Reward candor. While most people agree in theory that honesty is the best policy, too many bosses respond by blowing up if an employee candidly confesses to a mistake. For example, imagine a paralegal had been assigned to help an attorney file an important regulatory application for a client. The application deadline was coming up fast, when the paralegal admitted that he had failed to obtain a key piece of information that had to be included in the application. As tempted as the attorney might have been to dress down the paralegal, she saw that it would be smarter for her to work with him to salvage the situation, perhaps by helping him get the necessary information on an expedited basis or by formally requesting an extension of time. If the paralegal had been too afraid to admit to the attorney that the critical information was missing, the attorney would have been at risk of mismanaging the client's affairs by filing an incomplete application. While the paralegal's initial mistake was unfortunate, his candor in admitting to it deserves the attorney's praise.

This rule for making the workplace apology-friendly should be applied in both directions in the office hierarchy. Let's say, for example, your boss promised her boss that your department would complete a key project by the end of the week. Later she realized that the work couldn't be completed on time unless everyone working for her, including you, put in a lot of unscheduled overtime. Yes, your boss could apologize to her boss and deliver the project late, but everyone knows that her boss is a bit of a tyrant and that your boss could jeopardize her job if she did so. When your boss comes to you with an apology and a request that you put in several late nights, you have a choice. You can accept the apology grudgingly, making it perfectly clear that your boss offended you and that you won't let her forget it for a good long while. Or, if you're interested in promoting an apology-friendly workplace, your better choice would be to graciously accept her apology and cooperate in finishing the project on schedule. Your boss will likely notice, which may make things easier for everyone in the department the next time one of you makes a mistake.

Accept your own humanity. If you're in management, don't make the mistake of thinking that you can't ever admit to error. Far too many executives fear that if they admit to their staffers that they, too, make mistakes from time to time, the staff will lose respect for them. Nothing could be further from the truth. Your staff members are well aware of your shortcomings and blind spots, and can help you by pointing them out to you if you make it clear that they're welcome to do so. While that might not seem like a comfortable idea at first, honest feedback from your support staff can help you do a better job and produce higher-quality work for your clients and customers. Here's an example of one professional who learned that lesson:

Angela was an outstanding lawyer in many respects, but she was a terrible proofreader. A "big picture" person, Angela had trouble forcing herself to read documents word for word, and frequently failed to notice minor typographical and grammatical errors in her work. That created a problem for her, because she liked to produce most of her own documents directly rather than having someone else type them. As a result, Angela's otherwise careful and well-reasoned work tended to look a little sloppy, which eroded the confidence of her clients and professional colleagues.

Angela's administrative assistant, Linda, was nowhere near as well educated as Angela, but she was far more detail-oriented. One day, while retrieving from the printer a letter to a client that Angela had written, Linda noticed a typographical error and brought it to Angela's attention. Angela was a little annoyed that Linda had caught her in a mistake, but she thanked Linda and asked her to correct the letter. That encouraged Linda to start proofreading Angela's other projects, and she frequently found minor errors that she showed to Angela and corrected before the work went out. Angela quickly realized that, although her pride was sometimes a little hurt by what she considered to be Linda's nitpicking, the corrections that Linda made improved the professional appearance of Angela's work. After a little soul-searching, Angela recognized that proofreading wasn't her strong suit and that it didn't need to be. She came to deeply appreciate Linda's contribution, recognizing that Linda's proofreading made Angela look better to the outside world than she would have otherwise.

Accept other people's humanity, too. Your business associates may have unreasonable expectations of what you can do for them, or they may not understand exactly what you do. They may express themselves badly, overreact, or just have an off day now and then. If, for example, you work as a computer troubleshooter, odds are good that the people you work for have often called you in to fix a computer, and said something along the lines of, "This machine breaks down every five minutes! Why can't you just fix the @&*>#! thing so I can finally get some work done?" Be patient and, if you can, educate them a little. You don't need or want to turn them into computer experts, but it's usually a good idea to provide a layperson's explanation of what you're doing. Better understanding on their part can lead to more reasonable expectations and fewer angry exchanges later. Most important, do your best to let their ire roll off your back. Exasperation with a malfunctioning machine isn't personal, and even the most self-controlled people let frustration get the better of them sometimes. If you don't escalate the situation, you may even receive an apology later.

Make sure life goes on. Once a mistake has been discovered, an apology has been delivered, and amends have been made, incorporate any lessons learned from the incident, then get back on track as quickly as you can. Don't let the fact that you or someone else in your company made a mistake paralyze you. If you're in management, avoid the temptation to use an underling's error as justification to be unfairly critical or distrustful in the future. If you're one of the worker bees, show the people around and above you how well you can learn from a mistake by improving your future performance.

As Albert Einstein said, "Anyone who has never made a mistake has never tried anything new." If you can learn from your apologies, adjust your thinking, and move forward in a calm, professional manner, you'll teach your co-workers that mistakes aren't fatal. That will free them to admit their own errors, apologize as necessary, and solve problems without fear. Ultimately, your workplace will be a far more pleasant place, and everyone's work will improve.

The goal of creating an apology-friendly workplace is not to encourage laziness, careless work, or inappropriate conduct. If you find yourself dealing with an employee who is chronically late, rude, sloppy, disengaged, or dishonest, address the problems with that employee's performance as severely as you must. Just don't make the mistake of allowing your experiences with one unsatisfactory employee to poison the work atmosphere. For the vast majority of your company's employees, an apology-friendly workplace can provide reduced stress, more opportunity for creative thinking, better relationships with co-workers and customers, and improved morale.

CHAPTER 20

Working to Build an
Apology-Friendly World

Without forgiveness, there's no future.

—DESMOND TUTU

Sometimes it seems as though the world in general, and American society in particular, becomes less forgiving every day. A political leader makes one ill-considered statement, a pop star wears one unflattering costume, an athlete admits to doping a decade ago, and careers are destroyed, reputations are shattered, awards are withdrawn, and future opportunities disappear forever. An individual who attains fame and fortune is elevated to the level of a demigod for some period of time, and then gets put under the media microscope until his or her shortcomings are inevitably discovered. The former idol is then dragged down from the pedestal and into the mud. It's a predictable dance that is seemingly reenacted more frequently every year.

The regularity with which this cycle of exaltation and disgrace is repeated may be attributable to the media's insatiable appetite for scandal. In the communications industry, controversy sells, so a reporter or columnist who is eager to build a reputation may find it expedient to "spin" celebrities' foibles to make them seem more controversial. Since most people, famous and otherwise, make their share of blunders, it's not difficult to find something "shocking" to write about. The mistake becomes a scandal, the scandal becomes news, the pundits get involved, and a feeding frenzy results. The reporter's reputation is briefly made, and the celebrity's reputation is ruined. Does this process serve any positive purpose?

The existence of the Internet and the many social media sites that have sprung up with it haven't helped the situation. Thanks to cell-phone cameras, Facebook, YouTube, websites for all the major newspapers and magazines, and the 24-7 news cycle that constantly demands fresh fodder for the public's consumption, missteps that once would have been considered minor gaffes routinely explode into international scandals. Let's say, for example, that a voter poses a hostile question to a political candidate at a rally, and the frazzled candidate gives a rude or even profane answer. Years ago, the exchange might have been overheard by other people at the rally, and perhaps covered in the local paper. The candidate might have lost the election, but nobody outside the voting district probably would have cared very much. Now, however, we can practically guarantee that someone at the rally will catch the exchange on video. It will go up on YouTube, the electronic press will pick it up, and an ill-considered moment becomes a major news story—until the next time someone in the public eye says something offensive, and the focus shifts to him.

This whole blame-and-shame cycle gets even worse when a private person becomes the subject of a public scandal. There have been far too many tragic stories of children, teenagers, and young adults who have taken their own lives after their entirely human mistakes got caught on camera and plastered across the Internet. (Just the fact that the word *cyberbullying* exists suggests that we have a serious social problem.) Even if the victims survive the ordeal, it doesn't mean they haven't suffered harm. For example, it used to be common for college students to do stupid things, recognize the error of their ways, correct their mistakes, and grow up into professionally successful adults. Now employers routinely search the Internet for pictures and videos of job applicants behaving badly, which means a single wild party can effectively destroy a young person's professional prospects. Is society really better off this way? I think not.

I recognize that a lot of people take a certain dark pleasure in discovering the secret shortcomings of the rich and famous. Maybe they envy the successful and think it's only fair for the powerful to be brought low. Perhaps they want to believe that because successful people are fallible humans, they too could be equally successful despite their own failings. Unfortunately, though, I fear some people enjoy watching the rich and famous tumble into disgrace because they don't care that the former superstars are human beings who will suffer emotional pain as a result of their public ruin. In ancient Rome, gladiators were cut to pieces for the pleasure of the crowd. The Internet has become our new Coliseum, where people's reputations get skewered instead of their bodies. It may not be blood sport per se, but it's still a pretty ugly form of entertainment.

In my opinion, the cycle of adulation and humiliation that we play with our public figures and private citizens caught in the public eye will prove downright harmful over time. This is not to suggest that people should escape appropriate punishment when they deliberately break the law or run afoul of society's values, nor that they should be excused from making amends to the people they've harmed. However, it is unrealistic to expect politicians, musicians, athletes, actors, and business leaders (indeed, anyone) to behave like saints twenty-four hours a day, every day. The very ambition that permits prominent people to succeed is hardly likely to make them good role models for small children.

Some years ago, I happened to be in Europe when a scandal involving an American politician's ethical lapse became international news. One of the Europeans I met on that trip enjoyed a gentle laugh at my American expense. "A politician engaged in questionable behavior—it's hardly surprising, is it?" She suggested that Americans were, perhaps, a bit naïve to be so astonished by behavior that

Europeans all but expect from their politicians. As Lord Acton observed, "Power corrupts, and absolute power corrupts absolutely." In my friend's view, a powerful person's slip from the ethical pedestal might be disappointing, but it could hardly come as a surprise.

This story suggests that shock and outrage may not be the only appropriate responses to other people's mistakes. Perhaps our disappointment when our heroes fall should be tempered with a touch of realism. It may be that in utterly condemning our leaders when they prove to be human, we deprive ourselves of the opportunity to admire their achievements, even if we can't glorify every aspect of their personalities.

Any student of American history can tell you that some of our greatest leaders were riddled with human failings. Thomas Jefferson was a slave owner. Benjamin Franklin was a hard-drinking libertine by modern standards. Abraham Lincoln was a manic-depressive who suffered multiple breakdowns and business failures before being elected to the presidency. None of these men was perfect, but if any of them had been cast aside for his human shortcomings, America would have been far the poorer for it.

The time has come for America to take a more balanced look at its leaders and heroes, to revere their accomplishments and admire their strengths without demanding that they be free of human flaws. It might be wonderful if the most famous and powerful among us were, in fact, as perfect as we think we'd like them to be. Then again, if perfection ever becomes the only possible measure of success, the vast majority of us are doomed to fail.

Certainly, there are acts that are almost impossible to forgive. It would be very difficult to argue, for example, that the terrorists who attacked the United States on September 11, 2001, should be forgiven for the atrocities they committed. However, it's important not to treat every mistake another person makes as being as "unforgivable" as 9/11. Unless we as individuals can achieve and maintain a balanced perspective on what can and cannot be forgiven, how can any of us hope to be forgiven for our own mistakes?

Ultimately, America might be stronger and healthier if we would accept the fact that everyone, from the most powerful to the humblest among us, is going to come up short sometimes. We could then allow someone who made an honest mistake to apologize, make amends, and be accepted back among us. Sometimes, making amends may include returning money, going to jail, giving up power, returning awards, or apologizing to the American people for disappointing them. Once apologies have been delivered and amends made, though, society loses out if we continue to ostracize those who have the courage and humility to apologize for their mistakes.

The United States leads the world in many respects, and other countries look to us to be a beacon of hope and liberty in troubled times. Learning the art of the apology and demonstrating that Americans understand forgiveness could go a long way toward strengthening our relationships with other nations. So many of the conflicts that create violence around the world have their roots in long-standing grudges carried by warring groups that refuse to apologize and forgive. The United States is often called upon to be a diplomat for peace, seeking to negotiate reasonable compromises between angry factions. American diplomats would be that much more credible if they could demonstrate that we, the American people, know how to apologize effectively and accept apologies in turn.

Closer to home, American society's collective refusal to forgive celebrities' misconduct, and the cycle of exaltation and disgrace that plays itself out so often in the press, all too frequently percolates down to poison our businesses, our schools, our friendships, and our family lives. If we can't forgive politicians and celebrities we don't know, how can we hope to forgive our co-workers, business associates, friends, and family members? And if we refuse to forgive the people who are part of our daily lives, how can we expect them to forgive us in return?

Norman Vincent Peale once observed, "Resentment or grudges do no harm to the person against whom you hold these feelings, but every day and every night of your life, they are eating at you." He may not have been entirely correct in saying that a grudge does no harm to the person against whom it is held. Knowing that someone resents you or holds a grudge against you can be deeply hurtful, especially if you don't know what you did wrong or how to make things right. Peale was entirely right, however, in his observation that resentment and grudges eat away at the people who carry them. There may be some satisfaction in carrying a grudge, but it comes at a very high price.

If people can learn to apologize more effectively, perhaps, over time, American society as a whole will become less punishing, as more individuals come to appreciate the value of forgiveness. We're all human, and we all fail from time to time. Accepting that fact, and forgiving ourselves and each other when we make mistakes, frees us from the burden of anger and resentment. One unknown author wisely observed that the heaviest thing to carry may be a grudge. The sooner we learn to apologize effectively, the sooner we can put our grudges down and get on with the positive business of living.

Good apologies to you!

ACKNOWLEDGMENTS

English poet John Donne famously wrote, "No man is an island." Neither is any author, especially not this one! I'm deeply indebted to the many family members, friends, and business associates who contributed their apology tales to bring my abstract ideas to life. Your stories were profoundly personal and sometimes painful. I'm grateful for your generosity in sharing them and hope that I've managed to do justice to them.

Special thanks must go to my cherished friend Eric Kuzmuk for urging me to include a chapter on forgiving yourself that has become one of my favorites. Loving thanks go to my beloved Lance Landseadel, who suggested the chapter on learning from your apologies. It was a great idea from an amazing man, and it made the book more optimistic and helpful. Hugs and forever love go to my daughter, Tatyana. You've inspired and informed most of my ideas about apologizing to children and, along the way, you've taught me more about the joys of parenting than I could have ever imagined.

Thank you to my parents, Elaine and Larry Bloom, and to my brother, Steve Bloom, for all your love and support throughout the years that led to the writing of this book. Thanks to friends Michelle Brickwedde, Miranda Dedja, Ginger Hayes, Barbara Keddy, Carol Sears, Valerie Holt, Chris Robichaux, and especially Christine Sand Bluhm, for your encouragement and thoughtful comments on the manuscript when it was still a work in progress. It takes both courage and compassion to let an author know when something she's written doesn't quite cut it. That you delivered the message so kindly and honestly was truly a blessing for me, and probably something of a tightrope walk for you. Bless you for it!

And speaking of blessings, my deepest thanks go to my friends and literary agents, Peggy Keller and Ellen Kleiner of Blessingway Author Services. Their faith in the message of *Art of the Apology* and ironclad determination to bring it to a wider audience was deeply heartwarming and utterly humbling. Special thanks must also go to Scott Messina of MJF Books and Amy K. Hughes, both for believing in *Art of the Apology* and for your saintlike patience along the way. Your insightful editing helped me write a much better book than I could have on my own.

Lord Chesterfield once said, "An injury is much sooner forgotten than an insult." My biggest fear in writing these acknowledgments was that I would inadvertently fail to thank someone for their help, support, or encouragement provided along the way. For once, I'm going to break my own rule about using the word *if* when making an apology: If you're that someone, please take my omission as an unintentional injury caused by a faulty memory and not an intentional insult. I'm deeply grateful despite being forgetful, and I humbly apologize.